T0346966

good dog

by arinzé kene

good dog was first produced by tiata fahodzi in association with Watford Palace Theatre, receiving its world premiere at Watford Palace Theatre on 17 February 2017.

good dog

by arinzé kene

cast

Boy   Anton Cross

creative team

Director	Natalie Ibu
Designer	Amelia Jane Hankin
Lighting Designer	Zoe Spurr
Sound Designer	Helen Skiera
Vocal Coach	Mary Holland
Movement Coach	Annie-Lunnette Deakin Foster
Casting Director	Nadine Rennie
Film/Publicity Photography	TEAfilms
Production Photography	Wasi Daniju
RTYDS Assistant Director	Ajjaz Awad-Ibrahim

production team

Producer	tiata fahodzi in association with Watford Palace Theatre
Line Producer	Tara Finney Productions
Stage Manager	Naomi Brooks Buchanan
Wardrobe Supervisor	Mark Jones
Technical Tour Manager	Paul Thomas
Tour Technician	Chris May
PR	Chloé Nelkin Consulting
Marketing Associate	Yinka Aynide
Audience Engagement Associate	Danielle Baker

supporters

good dog would not have been possible without the support of:

Abigail Graham I Archie Graham I Arti Goyate I Ben Spiller I Bhavini Goyate I Cyril Nri I Danny Sapani I Edward Kemp I Emilyne Mondo I Garrick Trust I James Grieve I Janet Etuk I Janice Acquah I Jemima Levick I Jocelyn Jee Esien I Kobna Holdbrook-Smith I Lucian Msamati I Martin Cordiner I Matilda Ibini I Michael Storey I Orhan Nas I Rachel D'Arcy I Regional Theatre Young Directors Scheme I Roshni Goyate I Sabrina Mahfouz I Sharon Kanolik I Steven Downs I Stewart Melton I Vanessa Barbirye I Yomi Adegoke I 7 anonymous donors

and thanks

We would also like to thank:

Ajjaz Awad-Ibrahim I Calum Callaghan I Chris Atkins I David Carr I Desara Bosnja I Fehinti Balogun I George Balogun I Ivy Davies I Jaekwan Hunte I James Cooney I Janet Etuk I Joseph Adelakun I Lucian Msamati I Mitesh Soni I Rose Bruford College I Shola Adewusi I Yetunde Oduwale

cast

anton cross

Since graduating from the London Academy of Music and Dramatic Arts (LAMDA) in 2015, Anton Cross made his theatrical debut as Frank in the world premiere of Arthur Miller's *No Villain* (Old Red Lion). Anton was most recently a part of the Storyhouse company for their 2016 summer repertory season, where he led as Barney in a brand new stage adaptation of *Stig of the Dump* (written by Jessica Swale), as well as playing Le Beau and William in *As You Like It* and an Outlaw in *The Two Gentlemen of Verona*. Other theatre credits include *Stoney Fruit* (Fine Mess); *Elizabeth* (HighTide); John Blanke/Young Marlow in *She Stoops to Conquer*, Worcester in *Henry IV Part I* (LAMDA).

creative team

arinzé kene – writer

Arinzé Kene was named Most Promising Playwright at the Off West End Theatre Awards for *Estate Walls* in 2011, which was also nominated for Best New Play. Arinzé was named as a Screen International UK Star of Tomorrow in 2013 and was invited to take part in the Channel 4 Screenwriting Course in 2012. Arinzé was a member of the Young Writers' Programme and Writers' Super Group at the Royal Court Theatre and has been artist on attachment at the Lyric Hammersmith and the National Theatre Studio. Other writing credits include *God's Property* (Soho); *Little Baby Jesus* (Ovalhouse); *Wild Child* (Royal Court).

natalie ibu – director

Natalie Ibu is the Artistic Director of tiata fahodzi. For the company, directing credits include *bricks and pieces, i know all the secrets in my world, here* and *mango* (*tiata delights*, 2015).

Other directing credits include readings and productions at the Riverside Studios, Young Vic, Lyric, Southwark Playhouse, Southbank Centre, Jersey Arts Trust, The Old Vic Tunnels, Theatre503, The Gate, Latitude, HighTide, BAC, Òran Mór, Traverse, Royal Court, ATC at the Young Vic, OVNV at The Old Vic, Waterloo East and The Vineyard Theatre in New York, Royal Lyceum Theatre, Citizens', The Arches, Contact and Nottingham Playhouse.

Residencies include New York Theatre Workshop, the National Theatre Studio, Royal Shakespeare Company, Royal Court, Citizens' Theatre and Contact. She has been awarded bursaries from Regional Theatre Young Director Scheme, the Federation of Scottish Theatre, Scottish Arts Council and Arts Council East Midlands. Awards include Dewar Arts Award for Exceptional Artists Under 30, Time Warner Ignite 2, IdeasTap Innovator's Award and the Lilian Baylis Award for Theatrical Excellence.

amelia jane hankin – designer

Amelia Jane Hankin trained at RADA and the RSC. Recent design credits include *Torch* (Edinburgh Festival); *We Are You* (Young Vic); *bricks and pieces* (tiata fahodzi/RADA/Latitude); *The Neighbourhood Project* (Bush); *This is Art* (Shakespeare in Shoreditch); *The Tiger's Bones* (Polka/West Yorkshire Playhouse); *The Little Prince, The Red Helicopter* (Arcola); *Pinter's Triple Bill, The Crucible, Dealer's Choice* (Guildhall School of Music and Drama); *Rudolf, Night Before Christmas* (West Yorkshire Playhouse); *She Called Me Mother* (Tara Arts/national tour); *Fake It 'Til You Make It* (Traverse/Soho/national tour); *Horniman's Choice* (Finborough); *Mother Courage and her Children* (Drama Centre); *The Itinerant Music Hall* (Lyric Hammersmith/Watford Palace); *The Box* (Theatre Delicatessen); *You Once Said Yes* (The Roundhouse/The Lowry Nuffield/Perth International Festival, Australia); *The Many Whoops of Whoops Town* (Lyric Hammersmith); *64 Squares with Rhum and Clay* (Edinburgh Festival/national tour).

As Assistant Designer, theatre includes *A Midsummer Night's Dream, Death of a Salesman* and *The Christmas Truce* (Royal Shakespeare Company).

Amelia's designs for *The Itinerant Music Hall* were exhibited at the V&A Museum as part of the MAKE/BELIEVE UK Design for Performance exhibition.

zoe spurr – lighting designer

Zoe Spurr trained at the Royal Central School of Speech and Drama.

Recent theatre lighting designs include *The Truth* (Central Szinhaz, Budapest); *Muted* (Bunker); *Erwartung/Twice Through The Heart* (Shadwell Opera/Hackney Showroom); *The Knife of Dawn* (Sackler Studio, Roundhouse); *Affection*, *Hookup* (Outbox Theatre Company/Hackney Showroom/Contact Manchester/Site Specific); *Torch*, *This Evil Thing* (Edinburgh Fringe Festival 2016); *A Serious Case of the F*ckits*, *The Heresy of Love* (Central); *Bitches* (NYT/Finborough). Corporate designs include the Terry Pratchett Final Book Launch at Waterstones, Piccadilly Circus, and *Grey Goose Fly Beyond* at the Welsh Presbyterian Chapel, Shaftesbury Avenue.

helen skiera – sound designer

Helen Skiera was part of the original sound-design team for *The Encounter* (Complicite) and performed the sound live through UK and European tours, and Broadway.

As Sound Designer and Composer: *Here I Belong,* (Pentabus, UK tour)*; i know all the secrets in my world*, *The Epic Adventure of Nhamo the Manyika Warrior and His Sexy Wife Chipo*, *The Legend of Hamba* (tiata fahodzi/UK tour); *The Magna Carta Plays* (Salisbury Playhouse); *Harajuku Girls* (Finborough); *The Dog, the Night and the Knife*, *Pandora's Box*, *Sister Of*, *Miss Julie* (Arcola); *The Boy Who Climbed Out of His Face* (Shunt); *The Last Words You'll Hear* (Almeida/Latitude Festival); *Advice for the Young at Heart* (Theatre Centre); *The Centre* (Islington Community Theatre); *The Three Sisters*, *The Seagull*, *The Laramie Project* (GSMD); *Snow White*, *US/UK Exchange* (Old Vic New Voices); *Meat* (Bush); *Once in a Lifetime*, *The Eighth Continent*, *An Absolute Turkey* (E15)*; Colors, The Criminals, House of Bones*, *Medea* (Drama Centre).

As Associate: *Adler and Gibb,* (Royal Court); *I'd Rather Goya Robbed Me of My Sleep Than Some Other Arsehole* (The Gate).

As operator: *King Charles III*, *Chimerica*, *Jersusalem*, *Clybourne Park*, *Enron.* Helen has composed and performed music for websites and cabaret/comedy ensembles; and performed live on TV with Right Said Fred.

nadine rennie – casting director

Nadine Rennie has been Casting Director at Soho Theatre for the last ten years, working on new plays by writers including Dennis Kelly, Philip Ridley, Roy Williams, Shelagh Stevenson, DC Moore, Steve Thompson, Vicky Jones, Arinzé Kene and Oladipo Agboluaje. Directors she has worked with include Rufus Norris, Roxanna Silbert, Indu Rubasingham, Michael Buffong, Max Stafford Clark, Paulette Randall, Tim Crouch and Steve Marmion. Freelance work includes BAFTA-winning CBBC series *DIXI* (casting all three series to date). Nadine also has a long-running association as Casting Director for Synergy Theatre Project and is a member of the Casting Directors' Guild.

ajjaz awad-ibrahim – RTYDS assistant director

Having attended both the Brit School and a foundation course at RADA, Ajjaz Awad-Ibrahim graduated with a BA in Acting from the Academy of Live and Recorded Arts, where she became the first student to win The Lawrence Olivier Award Bursary (2010). Since leaving education, she has continued to develop herself as a theatre maker as well as an actor. In 2014, she debuted her children's theatre show *Bimwili and the Zimwi* at the Little Angel Theatre and assisted Melly Still for the Introduction to Directing course at the Young Vic. She then went on to write a short piece *Coffee? Cake?* which was performed at the Feminist Library to mark its 40th Anniversary, before being the Production Runner for *i know all the secrets in my world* with tiata fahodzi. In 2016, she returned to the Young Vic to be Assistant Director on *Parallel: Yerma*.

tara finney productions – line producer

Tara Finney Productions was set up to produce the critically acclaimed *Land of Our Fathers* which was Time Out's *Fringe Show of the Year* when it premiered in September 2013. The production transferred to Trafalgar Studios, toured nationally in 2015/16 and is currently available on BBC Arts Online. Productions include: *The Acedian Pirates, WINK* (Theatre503); *And Then Come The Nightjars* (national tour).

Tara qualified as a corporate solicitor before starting her theatrical career as Resident Assistant Producer at Theatre503 in May 2012. She then worked as a Producer for Iris Theatre and as Associate Producer for Company of Angels, before going freelance in July 2015. Tara also runs Tiny Fires Ltd with director Paul Robinson and their inaugural production, *My Mother Said I Never Should*, starring Maureen Lipman and Katie Brayben, received critical acclaim during its run at St James Theatre in spring 2016. Tara is supported by the Stage One Bursary Scheme.

naomi buchanan brooks – stage manager

Naomi Buchanan Brooks studied Drama and Theatre studies at Royal Holloway University and has worked in Stage Management for the past nine years. Recent credits as Company Stage Manager include *The Royale* (Bush); *Le nozze di Figaro, Alcina, Jenufa* (Longborough Festival Opera); *Romeo and Juliet* (Rose, Kingston). Credits as Stage Manager include: *Bug* (Found111); *You For Me For You* (Royal Court Upstairs); *Wars of the Roses* (Rose, Kingston); *King Lear* (Shakespeare's Globe); *Sunspots, The Mystae, Fault Lines, I Know How I Feel About Eve, Ignorance* (Hampstead Downstairs).

'...gorgeous theatre from a truly diverse company'
Lenny Henry, OBE

femi elufowoju, jr 1997-2010 | lucian msamati 2010-2014 | natalie ibu 2014-present

tiata fahodzi (tee-ah-ta fa-hoon-zi) –
a theatre company for Britain today and the Britain of tomorrow

Founded in 1997, our journey mirrors that of the British Africans we seek to serve; from early productions telling stories of emigration and diaspora (*tickets and ties*) to, under second artistic director Lucian Msamati, reflecting on the relationship Britain and British-Africans have with Africa (*belong*). In 2014 Natalie Ibu became our third Artistic Director and with her came a question: what does it mean to be of African heritage but of mixed experience? During her tenure, we continue to reflect the changing and developing diaspora with a particular interest in the dual and the in-between, in those who straddle worlds, cultures, languages, classes, heritages, races and struggles. It's in this – the messy, the multiple and the complicated identity politics – that tiata fahodzi sits, acknowledging that our audiences are more complex and contrasting than ever. Our work starts with the contemporary British African experience but reaches beyond to ask us all, what does it mean to live here, now?

staff members
Artistic Director and CEO   Natalie Ibu
Administrator   Bhavini Goyate

board members
Archie Graham | Stewart Melton | Edward Kemp | Emilyne Mondo | Janice Aquah

patrons
Lenny Henry OBE | Jocelyn Jee Esien | Jenny Jules | Danny Sapani

support us

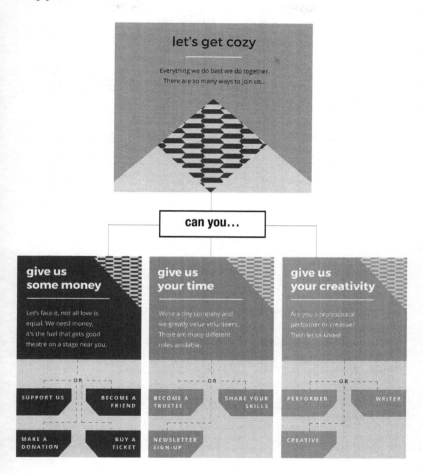

let's get cozy

Everything we do best we do together.
There are so many ways to join us...

can you...

give us some money

Let's face it, not all love is equal. We need money, it's the fuel that gets good theatre on a stage near you.

OR

SUPPORT US | BECOME A FRIEND

MAKE A DONATION | BUY A TICKET

give us your time

We're a tiny company and we greatly value volunteers. There are many different roles available.

OR

BECOME A TRUSTEE | SHARE YOUR SKILLS

NEWSLETTER SIGN-UP

give us your creativity

Are you a professional performer or creative? Then let us know!

OR

PERFORMER | WRITER

CREATIVE

We're a tiny company with huge ambitions and to realise our aspirations we need a little – well, a lot – of help from our friends.

Let's get cozy, email us at **fundraising@tiatafahodzi.com**

Supported using public funding by
ARTS COUNCIL ENGLAND

**Watford
Palace Theatre**

Is a 21st-century producing theatre, making new work across the art forms of theatre, dance, outdoor arts and digital, and developing audiences, artists and communities through exciting opportunities to participate.

Watford Palace Theatre commissions and produces plays from a range of new and established writers. Recent premieres include *Folk* by Tom Wells (in co-production with Birmingham Repertory Theatre and Hull Truck Theatre); *Wipers* by Ishy Din (in co-production with Curve Leicester and Belgrade Theatre Coventry); *Poppy + George* by Diane Samuels; *Coming Up* by Neil D'Souza; *Jefferson's Garden* by Timberlake Wertenbaker; *Love Me Do* by Laurence Marks and Maurice Gran; *An Intervention* by Mike Bartlett (in co-production with Paines Plough); *Shiver* by Daniel Kanaber; the Ideal World season of three new plays – *Perfect Match* by Gary Owen, *Virgin* by E.V. Crowe (in co-production with nabokov), *Override* by Stacey Gregg; *Jumpers for Goalposts* by Tom Wells (in co-production with Paines Plough and Hull Truck Theatre); *Our Brother David* by Anthony Clark; *Our Father* by Charlotte Keatley; and *Family Business* by Julian Mitchell.

Creative Associates are central to Watford Palace Theatre's vision these include Resident Company Rifco Arts and Creative Associate tiata fahodzi; Associate Companies Mahogany Opera Group; Scamp Theatre and Up In Arms; and Associates Kate Flatt; Shona Morris; Gurpreet Kaur Bhatti; Charlotte Keatley; Gary Owen and Timberlake Wertenbaker.

staff list

BOARD OF DIRECTORS
Deborah Lincoln (Chair)
Alex Bottom
Tola Dabiri
Cllr. George Derbyshire
Anne Fenton
John Hunt
Carol Lingwood
Binita Mehta-Parmar
John Pritchard
Georgina Rae
Brett Spencer
Patrick Stoddart
Gary Townsend Vila

Artistic Director & Chief Executive
Brigid Larmour

Executive Director
Jamie Arden

Communications Director
Dan Baxter

Administrator
Samantha Ford

Producer
Sophie Curtis

Buildings Facilities Manager
Sergio Steagall

Maintenance Technician
Brian Penston

Imagine Festivals Manager
Celine McKillion

Head of Finance
Andrew Phillips

Finance Officer
Tatiana Tiberghien

PARTICIPATION
Head of Participation
Hema Teji

Resident Director (Participation)
James Williams

Participation Projects Manager
Nicole Artingstall

Participation Assistant
Clare Hannington

Production
Head of Production
Matt Ledbury

Head of Electrics
Richmond Rudd

Deputy Head of Electrics
Francis Johnstone

Technician
Daniel Frost

Company Stage Manager
Maddie Baylis

Head of Stage
Chris Taylor

Wardrobe Supervisor
Mark Jones

Head of Construction
Tip Pargeter

Construction Assistant
Gillian Dessent

COMMUNICATIONS
Development Manager
Alisha Kadri
Marketing & Press Officer
Vanessa White
Marketing Officer
Cerys Beesley
Sales & Events Manager
Julia Yelland
Sales & Membership Assistants
Peter Shelton
Front of House & Bars Manager
Allen Gray
Cleaning Supervisor
Sharon Hunt
Cleaning Staff
Craig Ewer
Mohammed Fahim
Ankomah Koduah
Sandra Mjaisane

CUSTOMER SERVICE TEAM
Hamze Ali
Jhanky Baguandas
Morgan Bebbington
Conor Brownlee
William Burchnall
Myles Connaghan
David Cox
AD Dada
Kenny Dada
Tai Dada
Olivia Davies
Hannah Draper
Rory Duncan
James Dyer
Rhys Evans
Hope Feasey
Gemma Fisher
Lauren Foreman
Alycia Gaunt
David Gigney
Ben Henley-Washford
Kirsty Henley-Washford
Jessica Howes
Robbie Hunt
Mia Janes
Jodie Jenkinson
Jeanette Johnson
Brandon Jones
Kirsten Jones
Leo Jurascheck
Saskia Jurascheck
Josh Kelly
Sarah Kenny
Bradley Lawrence
Joe Learmonth
Dominic Levy
Fynn Levy
Laurelle Marfleet

Yvonne Marfleet
Lewis Marshall
Chloe May Ware
Collette Mead
Grace Meyer
Hannah Miller
Jess Moss
Teresa Murray
Isabel Nielson
George O'Dell
Alice O'Shaughnessy
Madeline O'Keeffe
Harriet O'Neill
Emily Pardoe
Aashi Parmar
Mark Pocock
Rita Reidy
Chloe Robinson Hunter
Evette Robinson
Annie Robson
Elliot Rosen
Valerie Sadoh
Layla Savage
Tom Scarborough
Sam Selby-Weatherley
Janet Semus
Ellie Shrimpton-Ring
Martin Spellman
Charlotte Spencer
Natalie Spencer
Maya Spencer-Jacobs
Doreen Tora
George Wakely
Charlotte Wallis
Jack Whitney
Tameera Williams-Simpson
Imara Williams-Simpson
Tom Wilson
Joseph Winer

Honorary Archivist
Ian Scleater

Creative Associates
Resident Companies
Rifco, tiata fahodzi

Associate Companies
Scamp, Mahogany Opera Group,
Up in Arms

Associates
Gurpreet Kaur Bhatti, Charlotte
Keatley, Gary Owen, Timberlake
Wertenbaker, Kate Flatt, Shona
Morris

WATFORD BOROUGH COUNCIL
BE BOLD

Supported using public funding by
ARTS COUNCIL
ENGLAND

Watford Palace Theatre is a
registered Charity No.1056950
www.watfordpalacetheatre.co.uk

good dog

arinzé kene

Character

BOY

This text went to press before the end of rehearsals and so may differ slightly from the play as performed.

one

I'm on the balcony pegging my school shirt on the line   hoping
for some late-afternoon sun so it dries before mum gets home
I look down where it's all happening

I see trevor senior park up   juss sit there   these times trevor
senior would sit there till the engine turns cold   I'll see his chin
drop to his chest and his eyes clamp up in there   it's like he's
sleep-talking cos his lips move   but he turns off the engine
unclips his homebase name badge   puts it in the glovebox
beside the other name badge for his weekend job   pulls out
that photo of his son posing with the red cricket bat   holds it in
his tough palm cos he's lived that tough-palm life   and his lips
start moving   but I clock what he's doing cos now he does the
sign of the cross   he's praying in there   praying dem heavy
blessings on his son   trevor senior was nuff worried bout his
son them times   cos of the incident that happened

whenever trevor senior finishes work late and gets in for the
hour that his son's in bed asleep   before he has his dinner
trevor senior likes to peek in his son's bedroom just to see his
chest go up and down one time   he was checking in on his boy
like normal   he open the boy's bedroom door   he nearly has
a stroke for what he sees   sitting on his son's bed   he sees one
duppy   juss there   his son's under the duvet asleep not
knowing   the duppy is sat there on his bed   iss back is to
trevor senior   it ain't juss a quick flash of the ting where ya
blink and iss gone   nah the ting's there jamming on the bed for
some time   trevor senior tries shouting at it to go away   nuffin
comes out   come like the duppy got some kinda invisible grip
around trevor senior's throat   his mouth juss hangs open   he
can't breathe   his cheeks are wobbling   his eyes are watering
iss only when trevor senior starts seeing dem floating bubbles
that you see juss before you faint that the duppy finally had
gone   allowing trevor senior to be free to collapse in the

doorway   to breathe again   and to venchually wake his son up
by crying on the floor like that   his son did join him in crying
too cos his son thought   *nah dad's going mad*   that scared him
obviously   cos trying to make sense of what his dad was
blubbering about was like

trying to find the bit to peel back on a roll of sellotape but there
being no bit to peel back   more frustrating the more it go on

trevor senior was trying to think how maybe he'd imagined it
cos truesay he was run ragged from lifting stockroom boxes
triple shifts back to back to back   and truesay juss some
moments before the duppy incident occured   as he shut his
kitchen window   there was a gush of wind   and some second-
hand weed smoke from outside did find iss way up his nose
but trevor senior thought nah nah nah   the duppy he saw was
real enough to go over and shake hands with   he swore to my
mum with his index finger skyward that the duppy left a crease
in the boy's duvet   of all the places in the yard the duppy
coulda sat   the ting chose his son's bed   so that worried trevor
senior   making him do weird fings like stand outside his front
door without putting the key in yet   he's doing it again   I see
him stood there ages screwing up his face at this fing   just
staring at this fing   man puts his bible on the wall   man puts
his tie on his shoulder   man squats down where there's nuff of
these fings on the ground there, picking up the fings   trevor
junior comes out now   thass the son   same age I am   trevor
junior doesn't ask no questions he juss leans his red cricket bat
against the wall   and bends down helping his dad picking up
the little fings there   shaking their heads   like it ain't the first
time they've done this   they both look at them little tings in
their palm   cos it's pure badness what dem lot do

there's someone shouting   so I look to the end of the block
where the stray cat runs out of gandhi's cornershop again
man's name ain't actually gandhi   no one knows what his
actual name is but someone started calling him gandhi one time
and now he answers to it   gandhi runs after the cat   got
a broomstick   barking suttin in his language   fuming cos
he can't seem to make the cat stop coming in his shop

problem is   gandhi got one of dem annoyingly slow-closing
shop doors   you know the door that when you try be polite and
shut it after yourself you tug it but it's nuff stubborn and wants
you to know that it's independent and is gonna shut itself in its
own slow time thank you very much   and you're like   *lissen
door I was only trying help you close cos you looked like you
were struggling so no need getting all independent on me*   and
you juss flick your hand away from its ungrateful handle and
leave it to take its time showing off isself   which unfortunately
for gandhi is juss enough time for that stray cat to slip in his
corner shop

so I watch gandhi chase the stray ting out into the street
swinging the broomstick   only in doing that   he abandoned
his post leaving the corner shop vacant   and behind him a
group of dem rude what what girls quickly slip into the empty
corner shop like   *awhaaat what what what what*   the what
what girls think they've got in without gandhi knowing but to
gandhi's credit   he fitted a jingle-jingle above that slow door at
the weekend   so he hears the jingle-jingle and spins around so
quick like in the cartoons making a doughnut on the pavement
with his cheap rubber bhs shoes   he dashes back to his shop
and kicks the what what girls out   they leave the shop like
*what what   what you mean I didn't buy nuffin   I didn't wanna
buy nuffin   I changed my mind   what*

them what what girls may not have bought nuffin   but as I see
them struttin down the pavement one panda pop come out of
one pocket and one *don't push me push a push pop* come out of
one pocket and one cheestring and one sunnyd juss appear from
nowhere and they're all drinking and chewing and bussing and
screwing as they walk past old man boateng

old man boateng is stood leaning against the wall as usual   in
his dusty old-man suit   wearing that ghanaian hat   it looks
like a bottle cap   obviously not the same size as a bottle cap
same shape I mean   it's held up by old boateng's ears   it's got
colourful little boxes like yellow and blue lego going round it
old boateng takes off this hat nodding for the what what girls as
they go by he compliments dem on the big hubba bubba bubble

gums they're blowing *yes   well done well done* he's always
complimenting people

I see him walk now   well he's kinda stumbling so he puts his
hand on the lamp post for balance   he looks to the end of the
road   there's a phone box there   he points at the phone box
he nods at the phone box   it's kinda far away for a stumbling
old man but regardless he takes one shaky step towards it
but of course   he's distracted because of   *jingle-jingle* gandhi
throws some flattened cardboard boxes out   he holds his
corner-shop door open for old man boateng to come in
old man boateng looks to the phone box at the end of the road
where he intends to go

two-two minutes later old man boateng is back there on his bit
of wall by the pavement   leaning gainst it   he did not make it
to the phone box   so with a shaky hand he sips that beer   but
he don't take his eye off the phone box   until mrs blackwood
walks past him   *that's a nice smile you have there mrs*
blackwood well done

mrs blackwood is on her way home from work   smiling
always smiling
she walks to her house   it's juss her and mr blackwood living
there but as mrs blackwood heads in she's surprised to find
marsha juss leaving   they cross each other in the door
ah marsha hello I dint know you were here
oh hello mrs blackwood my washing machine is having a break
oh right so you came to do your laundry at mine again
yes and mr blackwood been kind enough to let me do that
thank you
it's no bodder marsha it's what neighbours is for

marsha walks home   home for marsha is directly across the
road from the blackwoods   recently marsha been going over to
the blackwood house every couple days carrying a basket of
dutty clothes   cos her machine ain't good   but my mum say
that everyone cept for mrs blackwood know that marsha's
washing machine works perfectly fine   mum say it ain't to
wash clothes why marsha goes to mrs blackwood's   it's to
trouble mr blackwood why she really going there

next door   trevor senior with a palm full of dem little tings he's
picked up   has gone over to the four boys on the corner of his
house smoking   smoking on the corner of his wall   like they
always do   like it's their wall to smoke at   trevor senior's
talking to dem calmly like he always does   showing dem the
tings in his palm and then pointing at what they're smoking
he's asking if maybe they could not chuck their butts into his
front garden   one of the boys shrug   one of the boys laugh
one of the boys turn his back   then one other boy he got his
hoodie on backward   so the hood hang down on his chest
he looks like a joker   he's the only one who speaks to trevor
senior   *if am being honest big man it coulda been anyone*
lemme see it   firstly someone's obviously backrolled these
I'll say about backrolling   backrolling minimises how much
paper you use letting it burn slower   the benefit being a tastier
smoke   but backrolling's rare cos the backroll technique is
a devil to perfect   most heads struggle with tucking the glue
side round the little one-inch crutch   I've tried   it's stressful
truss   you gotta be mad surgical so it won't unravel by the time
you go to uh to lick it shut   but girls though   girls are
backrolling experts   girls got dem pencil fingers making it
easier to roll   plus girls obviously are more patient so uh
yeah I reckon some girls have been dashing these into your yard

trevor senior walks off and he's angry   but he holds it in   he
goes to trevor junior   tells him don't worry and rubs his head
he puts the red cricket bat in his son's hand   goes behind his
son   makes him stand with his back bent   with his legs a bit
open   they grip the cricket bat and together   really
slowly   they practise one swing

while dem four boys   on the corner of his wall smoking
laugh at dem
I hear barking

there's been a lot of barking   oh look   when I tiptoe I can see
into the two gardens over there   one garden's got that nippy little
dog with the big tail in it   the other garden's got that big dog
with the loud bark in it   big dog's constant barking is getting too
much though   neighbours have been complaining   but from

here I see who's got it worst   every time big dog barks   little
dog with the big tail in the garden next to it   shudders

ah man   my mum comin up the road my shirt ain't dry yet
an hour ago it had blue ink blotches all down the back of it
I cleaned it out but you can still see some of it   desmon's
handy work   sitting behind me in english   he spent most of
the period flicking his fountain pen on my back   worst fing
you can't feel the ink hit your shirt   iss only when you're
getting laughed at in the corridor when you realise

desmon got a problem with the fact that I ain't had no school
fights yet   he reckons that cos I keep turning fights down I'm a
weakling   this morning as he was tying all kinds of knots in my
school tie he said to me   *this is juss the way it's gonna go for you
cos from when you ain't nevah headlocked no one   from when
you don't know what it feel like to tense up your arm round a
person's neck from time to time   from when you only know what
the headlock feel like from the inside   you get tret this way*
then he walks me in a headlock all the way from the bus stop in
to registration   but that's nothing   that don't bother me   take
a lot more than that to bother me   I know sumfing them lot don't

desmon don't bother me   cos my dad told me from young how
important it is to be the bigger man   dad said   *when the time
come juss ignore them   let them laugh cos venchually
venchually the bigger man wins*   plus my form tutor pulled me
aside one time and done told me they're rotten   *dem boys are
rotten don't let dem spoil your character behave the way you
would if dey weren't boddering you and you'll do well toppa dat*
pastor clarence adds to this in church   the bible scripture
basically means that doing right and being good makes the
problems of life slow down and fade away venchally   the main
point dad form tutor and pastor clarence are making   is that
good things come to good people desmon don't kno the first
thing bout being good so no desmon I ain't accepting no fights
this week   cos I got good things coming   and I don't wanna
mess that up   if you wanna headlock me cos of that   fair nuff
do what you need to do you'll juss only be making me the
bigger man again

so in english when desmon kicks my chair and flicks my ear
I ignore him   ignore when desmon and his bredrin massive
martin bump me in the corridor   when they cuss my PE kit
arking if it's slim-fit   when they pull my trainer off my foot
throw it around the changing room   chat about how nike
wouldn't not put a tick on the side of it   *pay them no mind*
dad said   *and goodness will come for you   goodness gonna*
run you over   nuff sense that man spoke you know

so it's only goodness what I do   after school I always look both
ways before crossing as I breeze to the market before it close to
buy the things that mum gotta use for the catering she does
I walk past the corner shop and fight the crave to go in and eye
up the rows of sweets   cos I know thass only gonna make me
wanna use mum's change to buy one hubba bubba chewing gum
or one chupa chup lollipop   or one jawbreaker gobstopper that'll
last me till tomorrow   or one fat capri sun to suck till the carton
go skinny   nah I just blurt home with the shopping   drop
mum's change on the countertop   not one pee missing I help her
cook for whatever weekend event she's catering for before I do
homework   thass how am a good son   come the homework
I concentrate to do it right   cos truesay iss late and even though
am nuff tired and even though I hear dem lot living above going
mad at each other I know if I ignore that   concentrate   not spell
this wrong   remember to write my name on the top of the paper
cos I get minus a mark when I forget   and go to bed on time
even when mum's not round to check   I know the goodness that
comes when one is being good will come and run me over
mum'll get me that bike she promised me   it's the way it works

juss goodness all the way   even on the day of the lord   the
smoking boys and what what girls and desmon and massive
martin can snigger in the pews cos I dress well for god   and
after service when the church is empty   I am no stranger to
kneeling for the smaller jesus by the little candles   I pray for
people who got no drinking water   and I pray that desmon one
time might get to know what a headlock feel like from the
inside   not to spite him   juss so he can know that what he
does ain't nice   and I pray that mum hurry up and get me that

bike she promised   then after I pray wait patient for her to
finish talking to pastor clarence in his office

and on the bus home   I know not to agitate mum by asking
her   *when zackly you getting me the bike*   cos she did warn
me last time to   *stop asking about it bikes don't grow on trees*
she did say   *I'm saving for it*   and that was a while ago
before my last birthday and I still ain't seen no bike yet
ain't seen nuttin yet   everyone else got bmx bikes and sony
walkmans and nintendo 64s   but I know better than to
complain   cos being nuff nuff patient is being nuff nuff good
and if being nuff nuff good means

nuff nuff goodness will come my way   then one of these days
when I get in from school   I'll draw open that front door   and
boom   blinging in the corridor   so fresh and smelling like
new bike   I'll see it there   *what a bike mum   you got the* red
white and black bmx powerlite p24 cruiser   the one with free
agent pedals and maxxis holy roller tyres *that I dreamed about
thanks mum* I'm good at waiting cos   week after week on my
way home from market   I know not to stop too long outside
sam's bicycle shop eyeing up the ones waiting for fixing up
or the ones waiting for picking up   I don't really look   I might
look a bit and clench my jaw a little   but I don't really stare
I walk past it

mum comes through the front now   *why dint you come help me
with the bags you know the lift is broke*   she looks at my shirt
whass dat   she seen the blue stain   she walks toward me
no one said being good was easy   she blams me cross the head
and this goes on for weeks and weeks   cos desmon keeps
doing it   and mum keeps screwing about it   and this carry-on
for months and months   but I stay good

two

mum sends me to the shop cos she forgot to buy seasoning salt
as soon as I start walking down my road   I feel like I'm being
followed   I hear one of them playing super mario land the
gameboy behind me *duh nuh nuh maaario*   massive martin has
that game   I don't look behind me   I juss look forward and
walk   observing all dem lot who are being good so goodness
will come

I walk past the blackwoods' yard and I look in through their
window

mrs blackwood been good to mr blackwood   she's making him
food   she's always doing him a breakfast when he comes home
in the morning after his night-shift work then mrs blackwood
leaves out for work and she even holds her front door open so
that marsha from across the road can come in with her dutty
clothes basket   mrs blackwood even smiles at marsha and says
*wow your washing machine on a breakers again marsha   it's
what you wash in it – pavement slab?   it's where you buy your
machine from – one-pound shop?   it's what you replace the
fuse with – refuse?*   and they both laugh   until marsha shuts
the door on mrs blackwood's smile   but I see them now
through their window   mrs blackwood smiling as she gets in
from work   and marsha still there in her kitchen with mr
blackwood   marsha and mr blackwood laughing at a joke
a joke thass funny enough to bring tears to their eyes but one
that's no longer funny when mrs blackwood enter in the kitchen
mrs blackwood don't ask them what was funny   or why
marsha ain't gotten around to washing her dutty clothes yet
she juss smile that smile she got

cos for all her smiling   the goodness coming to her is gonna
be the one where mr blackwood's eyes will find her again   and
she'll be the one laughing out lungs with him like that in the

kitchen   like they used to do together   twenty-some years
back   when it was juss fresh   and they still had some rice in
their hair   when they planned to make a family   before they
found out it was juss only gonna be them two in that four-
bedroom yard for the next twenty

moah moah moah   mario juss died behind me   they're closer
to me   sniggering behind me and calling me out of my name
but I don't look back   all I gotta do is be a good son make it to
the shop buy seasoning salt for mum and go home

I juss carry on walking and I see that nippy little dog with the
big tail from one of the two gardens that I can see from my
balcony when I tiptoe   I see it trying not to fret when that big
dog barks   I see that little dog with the big tail clench up itself
and look at its own reflection in the garden-door window
telling itself   *come on   you're juss gonna have to get used to
this nutter barking loud and all the time   big dogs are gonna
bark loud and all the time   thass what they do   so stop getting
shook y'understand   truesay big dog ain't even done anyfing
deep to you   truesay it ain't you that big dog even barking at
truesay it ain't like big dog trying leap over the fence or nuffin
man up!*

yeah man   truesay desmon and massive martin might be cussin
from behind me   but truesay they ain't trying to tump me down
or nuttin   that little dog gives me strength not to turn around
and I carry on and head into gandhi's corner shop

even gandhi been good to someone   he's letting the stray cat
be in his corner shop   it's juss there on the floor and gandhi's
smiling about it   he tells me he clocked that whenever the stray
ting come in the shop   it always makes a beeline for the hole
by the skirting board where the rat and mice that eat up half his
shop come out   *all this time stray cat been coming in here to
genocide these mice for me and I've been chasing it out you
know*   I watch gandhi as he watches the stray cat sit there by
the hole   its the first time I see him not look vex   but the good
mood don't last long

a what what girl comes in and tries teefing one fifteen pee
curly wurly   *awhaaat curly wurly whaaat get off my arm*

gandhi dashes her out his shop   two-twos later now gandhi's
slow door gets kicked with a force that makes it fling open quickly
that what what girl's mother busses in and goes mad flinging up
her arms and raising up her voice   *oh you calling my daughter*
a teef gandhi   you calling my daughter a teef   don't fink I don't
notice everything in your shop says nottobesoldseparately gandhi
don't make me have to tell everyone to boycott your shop
boycott your shop did make gandhi's ears shoot up like the stray
cat he'd been studying juss moments before   and while the what
what mum continued scream down his shop gandhi's in his head
doing math sums thinking   *hmm   nuff of dem what what girls'*
parents come to my corner shop daily   if I bans one   they
boycotts my shop and I lose the lot   thass what what   twenty-
two   twenty-five customers not buying   cigarettes milks eggs
fruits vegs tv guides   the sum of gandhi's thinking made him
without arguing back   stand up   go to his fridge   grab two big
sunnyds   give one to the what what girl   and one to what what
mum   *next time you come I'll give you discount*   and he nicely
holds the door open for dem to go

man like gandhi ain't in the business of losing customers
when I put my seasoning salt on the counter all the calm he juss
displayed is nowhere to be seen   man's punching numbers in
the register with a madness   telling me   *corner shop is tricky*
business iss juss one irn bru bar and one cherryade and one
vimto bar they take once a day   iss cheaper to let dem steal
than lose customer   but then they have no respect for me
sumfing in my language sumfing else in my language   gandhi
slides over my change and before letting me take it   asks me
what do you think I should do

I grab my seasoning salt   gandhi   I think you should always
do what is good   *wot's good*   I don't know yet gandhi   cos
am thirteen   but am working on it   if you get there before me
lemme know   either way they'll get what coming to dem   but
I don't think you should give dem no free sunnyd   remember it
turnt a girl orange gandhi

I walk out of gandhi's shop and fall smack on my face   cos
desmon sticks his leg out tripping me up   I hear a pop when
I land and there's something under me

ah man   the bag of seasoning salt   mum's gonna kill me
half of it is on the floor it's gone past the five-second rule
so I juss take my half-bag and carry on walking   dem lot
laughing behind me

I pass old man boateng leaning on his wall   he's got a drink in
his hand   he's looking at the phone box at the top of the road
he compliments me   he's always complimenting people   he
sways back and forth as he tells me   *well done for being*
mature   other children will be crying but you juss pick yourself
up and walk   well done   but every now and then it's ok to cry
son   you're only young once so you can act your age and cry
and run around and eat sweets   you never eat sweets   you
walk up and down here sweetless   children should eat sweets
I loved sweets   I used to wake up at four thirty every morning
to help the milkman with deliveries   and all of my earnings
would go to sweets   I'd eat it until I had tongue ache   then
one day I juss got bored and stopped eating sweets   juss like
that   that's why you should have sweets   get it out of your
system   I know that's what will happen with this   he sips his
beer and raises it   *one day I'll get bored of this   one day I'll*
be walking up this road and I'll suddenly be at the phone box
and I'll laugh and say   haha
I walked straight past gandhi shop without even looking at the
fridge   then I'll take the change out of my pocket   and make
that phone call   0181…   0171…

walk past trevor senior's place   he out there practising cricket
with trevor junior as usual   smoke is blowing their way   I can
see trevor senior trying to keep a cool head being a good
example for trevor junior   but them smoking boys don't make
it easy for him

trevor senior ain't seen the duppy since that night   but he
wonders if iss placed any curses around   iss burning him
wondering what the duppy visit meant   makes him worry to
the point where iss rotting his mind   he keeps a close watch on
trevor junior as they're out front practising   smoke blowing
their way

police   they only swing by these bits   keep it brief   even
when they do swing by   them smoking boys see them coming
from a distance and move away   then return later   trevor
senior hopes that one day   some smarter police guys   will
reach the corner of his house without the smoking boys
knowing   and make them move off that corner   so that he and
trevor junior can practise out there with no smoke blowing in
their eye   trevor senior won't call them police though   cos if
you call them   you're asking for a whole bag of problems
cos even though you done told them   *do not come to my door*
I've seen it nuff times   they still wanna knock on your door
and ask you why you phoned   smoking boys will see it's you
who called   and they'll tip your bin over every day and blame
it on the fox   crack your kitchen window with a stone an blame
it on the wind   trevor senior knows it's best he let the law
come when they come   he's juss being good

mum's been good too   I get home and I hear her praying
keep him in your protection   she's praying for dad   *even
though true he's gone back home for business at a time when
yes everyone from back home wanna come here for business
I juss know that if you keep him in your blessings and your
favour dear lord   he'll find the contract he's been after and
then come back to us   I very often give offerings at church lord
I know you see me   I do one on ones with your very own
messenger pastor clarence after mass dear lord   so let me be
happy again   let your will be done now…   why's there blood
coming down your elbow   come here   that my seasoning salt
what you mean you fell over   you wanna interrupt my prayer
with this   come here   come here*

and mum tells me iss for my own good   so I understand the
value of money   so that I'll be more careful next time   iss for
my own good   everyone's being good

three

iss the first day back to school after chrissmas and new year
I wanted a bike

other kids in my area got sony cd walkman from currys or sony
playstation from comet   but I got this tamagotchi dog
bleepbleep bleep bleep   it come like second nature now
being the bigger man

I'm ready for school   I pass mum's bedroom and she ain't in
there   more often now I see her knelt there with her elbows on
the bed   praying that she want something to make her happy
she want a piece of happiness inside her   she was happy last
night   she got in late   she was alone but I heard her talking
and giggling   bumping into things in the living room   falling
over laughing   she had happiness in her last night   but then
the laughing stop   I heard crying

I pack my lunch and I tiptoe around mum on the living room
floor   try not to wake her   I slowly raise up her head   to grab
my school shoe from under it   and slide one soft cushion there
in its place

iss nuff cold out   on my road nuff people are still being good
like mrs blackwood   I see her walk across the street to marsha's
and knock the door   *morning marsha   I'm juss about to do
some washing and an idea came to mind   I could save you the
effort of coming round later while I'm at work   because it's
nearly every day now that you come isn't it*   marsha gives mrs
blackwood her dutty clothes and mrs blackwood walks home
smiling that smile

I walk past old man boateng   where before he lean up against
his wall   this past year something keep pulling him down from
that wall

old man boateng juss   lies on the pavement now   face down
and spread out   and these times it's bare cold   people juss

stepping over him all day   one of them smoking boys might
stand him up if his trousers ain't dripping wet somehow   but
he always slides back down after

I try pick him up but he's too heavy so I juss sit him up   *well
done well done   thass a nice key ring you got   it's making noise*
it's a tamagotchi from woolworths   a digital pet that is also a key
ring   *bleepbleep*   that means I gotta feed it   iss a dog *yep well
done very nice dog* if I don't feed it then it'll die   I've kept it
alive for two weeks now he's staring   over my shoulder at the
phone box   *when I'm ready   when I stop wanting the drink like
what happened with the sweeties   I'll be in the phone box   I'll
make that call   call my daughter and I'll say   who's that in the
background   she'll put my grandchildren on   and set up a time
I go meet them   bleepbleep*

I walk past the garden where that little dog with the big tail is
I peep in through the gap in the gate   man   where before all
big dog from the next garden did was bark loud   now it come
right up to the fence   sticks its face into the gap where a piece
of wonky fence had slid down after one windy night   and it
barks straight at little dog   making him shook up

what's worse is that where before little dog with the big tail could
escape the madness   could run away into the house into the
kitchen   and not have to hear the bark as loud from there   now
little dog's owner is gone out most the day   locking little dog in
the garden   for it to get bark at through that gap in the fence all
afternoon   so now when owner comes back   little dog don't
even let owner open the garden door fully before it blast itself
indoors   thass the torment of the whole mess   *bleep*

all little dog ever wanted   was to run around the garden with
freeness   but it's juss barking madness what it gets every day
now   little dog used to like to dig some holes there from time
to time   but with this new stress level   little dog can't even
take a piss the way it used to   instead of one streaming piss
little dog now pisses in short squirts between barks   it takes the
pleasure out of it   it's the same for pooing   moretime little
dog spends the night holding half a painful shit in him   and it's
nuff cold

I get to school now   first day back   soon as I bop through the
gates desmon pulls me around by my tie   him and massive
martin walk me around the school by my tie like it's a dog show
in class when I'm writing he shoves my desk and makes me
draw a fat line across my work   *bleepbleep*

desmon's still flicking my ear and kicking my chair   teacher
calls my name so I stand up and read my homework out loud
bout what I done over the holidays   them lot laughing at the
mistakes in my english   I don't backchat them   cos in
arguments my voice gets so shaky and loose and when I hear it
so weak like that it surprises me and makes me more upset
I carry on reading through the lump in my throat   and they
keep laughing cos I ain't good at reading out loud   *man can't
read   man can't even read the ting and he wrote it*   sometimes
I feel like the words are playing tricks on me   they're bussing
up and rolling over and smacking palms on their tables and
holding their chests   some of dem with tears coming down
gripping their ribcage saying they can't live   teacher shouts at
me to sit down like I intended to disrupt the class   I sit back
down but desmon moved my chair away so I fall to the floor
and roll back and my legs swing up in the air

I sit in my chair   my body feels hot   *bleepbleep*   desmon
starts flicking my ear again   and my eyes feel loose like
they're floating in warm water

no one said being good don't come with pressures   but when
I think of dad's words   *goodness gonna mow you down and
swerve round them*   and when I think of the brand-new bike
thass coming to me   when I think of my church clothes
blowing back as I glide down the hill riding it   then I can't feel
my ear being flicked any more

come play time I don't stand in the hall cos some heads wanna
bump into me   I don't like the football cos some heads blast
the ball at me   don't like going to the tuck shop cos some
heads wanna push in front of me in the queue or push me to the
back of the queue or push me out the queue altogether

so I go library   steady my eye to read something   cos it's not
that I can't read   it's juss that when I do   no sentences make

sense until the third fourth time I read it   cos my eye can't
keep steady   wants to leap over a word without my permission
or put this word before the other one   or have this sentence
take on one of the words from the sentence underneath   so
moretime I'm in the library juss steadying and training my eye
to not skip words   to only skip the words I don't know   but
also I'm here to hide

jamilla is always here reading   before school   at lunch   and
after school till the library closes   she sits at the desk in the
corner facing the wall   her head down   she moves like a ghost
library to class   class to class   class to library   library to home
I've never actually heard jamilla speak   when people speak to
her she don't speak back   like when she's walking in the hall
and the what what girls say to her   *whaaat jamilla why you*
always smelling like b o   whaaat look at that brown ring round
your shirt collar   why your nose so runny   why your eczema
spreading like wildfire   with your neck all skinny like cheestring
I ain't ever seen you eat nuffin   do you even eat jamilla

they might stick one rude note to her back without her knowing
or stick one foot out to trip her over   but jamilla juss ignores it
I respect her for that   cos dad always said   *when you don't*
give them the satisfaction then you get the satisfaction

bleepbleep

after school on my walk home   I see jamilla's dad through the
window of the betting shop   gripsin a piece of paper in his fist
and staring up at the screen   he's been in there every day this
week   gripsin a paper   then gripsin his head

passing gandhi's shop I see he's put a sign in is window saying
only two what what girls allowed in my shop at a time   but
then I see them what what girls storm in ten of them at once
and in the few seconds it takes gandhi to run from behind the
till and chase them out   the damage is already done   I watch
him through that slow-closing door   looking at his shelves and
yelling at himself   *before it was juss a couple twix   couple*
wine gum   couple hoola hoop they teef   now iss whole box of
frosty corn flake   whole family-size packet dorito   whole
multipack rich tea and bn bns they teef   they teef everything

cept the shelf   gandhi stomps around and pulls out his beard
complaining that what the what what girls don't teef   the rats
and the mice get to   and the way that rats shred up the
packaging of things   it makes some packets harder to reseal
and resell than others

I've seen what he does though   gandhi can't afford to throw
food away   so what can't be resealed he pours it on the floor in
the corner   and stray cat yams it up   stray cat lives there in his
shop now full time   even though gandhi's always cussin it   *this
whole year stray cat you ain't killed no rat no mouse no nuttin
mostly you juss curl up to sleep   that ain't what you're hired for*

still   with all the teefing gandhi ain't ban a single what what
girl from his shop   man ain't in the business of losing
customers   take old man boateng for example   old man
boateng can't always make it to the shop   sometimes his legs
are too wobbly to take him   so gandhi lets him send a smoking
boy to buy for him no matter their age

gandhi knows that as long as he don't lose customers   he'll end
up more successful than his two younger brothers who have
teased him all his life   and gone into business with each other
making nuff money   gandhi's too busy to feel bitter about that
he knows that as long as he keeps customers   then when his dad
comes england to visit   his dad won't be able to deny that his
fifty-one-year-old boy   is a man who made it   in great england
his dad'll even start to visit him as often as he visits his brothers
in dubai   if not more   *bleepbleep*   I carry on walking

I see trevor senior's still trying to make a banging cricketer out
of trevor junior   smoking boys don't make it easy for him
though   where before it's three or five of them out there   now
it's steady twelve or fifteen out there all hours   it ain't juss the
smoking thass bad   when they're out there practising   trevor
senior gotta tell his son to close his ears   the things them boys
say on a regular   disgusting things   and trevor senior can't
shoo them cos they live here too and some of their parents are
decent people   but trevor senior been looking at them smoking
boys through the corner of his eye of recent   like he might juss
tell them something soon

thing is   trevor junior needs that space outside to practise now
more than ever   he's getting older   and he's a good cricketer
but he needs to get scouted   trevor junior ain't that clever on
paper   ain't gonna make no doctor or lawyer   so his dad
worries bout his future   worries that if he don't make a
banging cricketer outta his boy soon   his boy might not have it
in him to make anything outta himself ever   trevor senior
worries trevor junior might end up like him   living that tough-
palm life from doing them jobs where you gripss and draipss
tings around   worse even   he worries trevor junior might end
up like them smoking boys

so through all the cloud smoke   and the dutty joke   the trevors
practise hard   maybe too hard   trevor junior don't look to be
enjoying it the way he used to   but the way trevor senior sees it
something good gotta come from all this good practice

I carry on home and suddenly there's nuff flowers on the floor
that I gotta be stepping over   and I accidentally kick one
flower   and one neighbour juss runs forward at me and bring
up her arm like she wanna chop me down   tears in her eye
but someone holds her back while she tell me I got no
respect   she puts the flower back straight again on the floor
and everyone's juss standing around in quiet   wagging their
chins slowly   and now I know   why we're all stood here in
the cold

man never got to the phone box

after all the complimenting   and raising everyone's spirit   not
being a bother to no one   being kind   being good   man didn't
make it past the corner shop

and I juss think to myself   we all loved him   if a good person
as safe as old boateng   went away before his problems did
how then   can I know for sure   I'll get to ride down a hill

this feeling come to me   feeling of doubt   wondering   if being
good   being nice   gets rewarded properly   I look around and
truesay everyone trying to do good is struggling   the ones
laughing and grinning are the marshas   and dem what what girls
and dem smoking boys   and dem desmons and massive martins

made me not sure if after being nuff patient bout our problem
keeping a tight face bout our problem   if we get rewarded any
better than the problem-makers   the good ones are stressed out
right now   I already know iss harder to be good   but is it
worth it   after all the stress   is it worth it in the end
bleepbleep   what's the point in feeding this ting and taking it
for walks and dat

I get home and mum sits me at the table   she's smiling
maybe she don't know yet bout old man boateng   she's smiling
and truesay this smile is a real smile   I ain't seen mum smile
like this since dad was here   so I'm thinking   *is dad coming
back*   she tell me she don't know but that she's happy   so I'm
now thinking well it's the bike it's gotta be the bike innit she's
finally saved up   *let's get that bike tomorrow*   I'm juss
waiting for her to say that so I can dash this tamagotchi away
she tells me she's happy   and I'm betting she's happy enough
to order me one argos bike over the phone right now   my eyes
go to the cupboard where the argos catalogue is   page three-
seven-four is where there start being bikes   *joy   happiness
and life is inside me*   she says   *a blessing from god in me
and it's growing every day   but it takes a lot of my energy
I can't work like before   I'm gonna need you to be a big boy
you hear me   to go market and cook more times a week   you
know all the shops well now*

mum goes upstairs to rest   in my head I replay everything she
juss said   checking if she mentioned a bike and I missed it
even if I did get my bike   when now would there be free riding
time   the doubts are in me   swelling up

I reach for my homework   but my mind won't steady   cos am
full up with doubt   ruining me   *be good   be good and
goodness is gonna*   doubt   it twiss and tangle up in me   *be
good for what*   the doubt making me hate myself for being
good all this time   feel like I been a fool   goodness don't
know what iss doing in me any more   all that good behaviour
I've been stacking   don't want it in me no more   has to come
out   it drops out   small at first   on to my work book
softening the paper   then flows outta me on to my page   and
when I write on the page   it rips   am writing on it juss to rip it

cos I did everything I was spose to do   still there's no goodness
running me over   cos it don't work that way   and it don't
make no sense to me   it's like I been turning this roll of tape in
my palm for ages   concentrating on it   they told me there was
a bit to peel back   but they lied   there's no bit to peel back

I go to the balcony   more flowers getting put down for old man
boateng but everyone's kinda standing around talking in little
clumps now   trevor senior and trevor junior in the back still
practising   trevor senior bowls and trevor junior bats   the ball
then hits the wall on the side of their house   then it'll hit about
three other fings before it's ready to slow down   hits the wall
then the floor   then rolls and hits a curb   bounces off the curb
and hits a tyre   then it'll get nuff slow and stop   back to normal

I watch this   and I think of when I get hit   thinking   what if
I'm like the ball   all these problems I keep getting hit by
what if what I need to do   in order to get myself back to
normal afterward like the ball   is to pass on the hit the way the
ball does

I mean   juss imagine the ball had nothing to slow it down   no
wall no gravity   nuttin   it would juss carry on forever   I'd
juss carry that hit in me forever   carry that problem   with
nothing to pass it on to   no one to pass it on to

I watch   as trevor junior hits the ball and the ball hits the wall
then off the wall it bounces and hits one smoking boy in the
shoulder   knocks the smoke out his hand   it's the boy who
wears his hoodie on backwards   the hoodie resting on his chest
his boys are laughing at him   he ain't laughing   everyone's
looking now everyone who's gathered for old man boateng
smoking boy tells trevor junior to   *come here and pick up my
smoke*   trevor junior don't move   or can't move   smoking
boy tries a next tactic   he balls both fists and moves toward
trevor junior with a coldness   thass when trevor senior juss
switches   he grabs the red cricket bat off his son   raises it up
screaming   he runs at the smoking boy like he's gonna hit him
with it   the boy runs back to his boys   but trevor senior still
runs at them   so now they all dust down the road   legging it
with trevor senior behind them giving chase   swinging the bat

juss missing their backs   them boys run all the way down the
road past the phone box   trevor senior stops   watches them
disappear   then walks back   there's tears in his eyes   but he
and trevor junior juss carry on practising   all the neighbours
stand there frowning

but I smile   cos iss making sense now   juss like the ball
them smoking boys hit trevor senior with a problem   he
couldn't juss carry the hit   he had to pass it on

some neighbours start chatting to each other now saying   *if you
chase them away with a cricket bat thass stooping to their level
makes you juss as bad as them   trevor senior shoulda handle
hisself better   thass not how you solve problems*   all this is
coming from neighbours who ain't yet figured out how to solve
their own problem   they saying   *what he done ain't proper
more problems are made that way*

but there ain't no truth to that   more problems don't come
bleepbleep   I let my tamagotchi die and no problem come   and
no problem come for trevor senior cos come the next day them
boys ain't there smoking on the corner of his house   I watch
them use up all the space to practise   same thing the day after

so maybe iss like the ball I gotta be   like a ball thass been
bashed   if something bashes me   I bash things till I calm
down again

25

four

in class we're doing comparative adjectives for creative writing
people stand and give answers like   *fast faster fastest   cold
colder coldest*   I'm distracted looking out the window at the
PE group playing cricket   *long longer longest*   I ain't thought
up what I'm gonna say by the time it's my turn   I stand up   *uh
good gooder nah   bad baddest   worse worster   best better
bettest   the best   bestest*

the class are in tears   the teacher pretends to write something on
the board but her shoulders vibrating give her away   desmon
stands up   desmon quiets everyone   *shut up you lot I got one*
desmon points to me   *dumb dumber dumbest*   the class go
mental   *it's right though innit missis   dumb dumber dumbest*

I sit down   around me are people falling on their backs   arms
wrapping their ribs shaking their legs in the air   out the
window a red ball hits the fence

aahhhhhh   ahhhhh   aahhhhh   aaaahhhhh   I fling my chair
back   push my desk forward   storm out the door   slam it
behind me

and guess what   no teacher drags me by my blazer to the
head's office   no talks of calling home   no threat of detention
I did it   I passed the hit on   to the chair and the desk and the
door   before I'd carry the hit   but I feel good now

there's a new person in me straight away after that   he walks
down the hall with this new limp   he don't tuck in his shirt
he ain't trying to be good

this new me goes to the library at lunch   rip my sangwhich in
half   and share it with jamilla   put my arm across the back of
her chair   brush knees with her   I don't care that she smell
like b o   I don't care bout the brown ring on her shirt colour
and even when desmon and massive martin draips me out that

chair   drag me out the library and into the hall   to rearrange
my face   cos no one gets away with slamming a chair into
desmon's desk   this new me   takes the battering with pride
cos with this new way of being   I don't juss curl up in a ball to
get kicked around like a empty dr pepper bottle in the
playground   I get a few good digs of my own in when there's
an opening   I don't get tie-walked and made to jump through
no fire tyre   I ain't a dog show no more

jamilla helps me stand up when desmon and massive martin are
done   and as we walk down the hall   juss in case there's a
doubt in my mind about the new me   since after getting
battered   I ain't faking the limp

and at lunchtime   I wait in line at the tuck shop   keeping my
place by not fraiding no one   when they try push in front of me
I juss budge up nuff tight with the person in front leaving no
gap   and I buy that small pack of haribo mix and give the
hearts and rings to jamilla

come after lunch we're in science   and desmon's behind me
but he ain't flicking my ear   he's nuff quiet   staring out the
window at a black car thass been parked there

by the school gates   when two men come out of the car and
head to the main entrance   desmon raise up his hand to go
toilet   but he don't go toilet   he don't return to class

when class is done teacher tasks me with taking desmon's bag
to the main office   as I cut through reception   and I see
through the window   desmon being put in the back of that
black car by the two men   handcuffs on him   his eyes are red
his lips are puffy

I take desmon's bag to main office   but not before looking inside
it and liberating his nike hi-tops and the rolled-up cigarette

as I hand his bag in I overhear   the school nurse   the secretary
and one supply teacher   whisper about desmon   *he did it
before he left for school this morning   took a screwdriver to his
dad   left him there bleeding   he's in hospital in stable
condition he'll be ok   desmon won't be ok though I don't
reckon   yeah I agree   I agree too   he's been in trouble too*

many times before   let off nuff times before   but know what
what   I reckon iss his dad who starts it   totally agree   yeah
iss his dad   cos remember that time   the car park   after
parents' evening   what happened   well   don't think he was
happy with the report desmon got his dad   I dint see anything
actually happen but remember   yeah we saw desmon holding
his head   his dad sped away   leff him there holding his jaw
side   holding it like it was gonna fall if he let go of it   we ask
if he's all right and what happens   tells us to f-off don't he
nearly had a go at us   he's known to the law   been before
judges nuff times before   this time he won't get a slap on the
wrist   yeah I agree   the officer said he's going young
offenders and I bet he's right   I agree   yeah me too   we all
agree   may as well take him off our registers

after school I smoke the roll-up   it ain't a normal cigarette   iss
what them smoking boys smoke   it makes me feel lucky   so
lucky that I put on desmon's nike hi-tops   and I walk them
home   some people ask me how come I got desmon's crep and
I walk pass them I say   *I took them off of him   I caught him*
slipping   gave him da bam bam one two tumps that made
echoes in his hollow chest   made dat boy run barefoot

thass what I tell them   cos I know he ain't gonna be back to
make me prove it   I got these fresh nike hi-tops on but I'm still
limping on my way home

then I see this brudda   a brudda my age   walking on the other
side of the road   going the other way   one side of his school
shirt untucked like me   bit of fresh blood on that shirt like me
cos he probably got licks like me   he's limping a bit when
walking like me   he raises his chin to me as we're passing
I raise mine back   but iss all too strange   too much of a
coincidence   so I turn round to see if he finds it weird too
but the brudda ain't there   brudda juss gone   like a duppy

five

Desmon's nike hi-tops don't fit me no more   grew out of them
besides I'm on the balcony and I look down at the smoking boys
and everyone's wearing leather avirex jackets now   yeah they've
come back to the corner   texting on their t-mobile chips with
their blackberry bolds   voices deeper   eyes are deeper   I'm
here smoking   topping up that lucky feeling   I look across and
I ain't got to tiptoe to see the two gardens any more

I see that little dog with the big tail got a new problem now
the problem is iss own big tail   over the years little dog has
loved iss big tail cos chasing it in circles gives little dog plenty
of dizziness   but little dog now wishes it was born with a short
one like other dogs iss size

some days ago little dog was in the garden chasing iss big
tail   when without warning little dog hears a shaking at the
fence   little dog stops and turns around to find big dog from
the next garden stood juss some dog feet away   iss big
shoulder and leg muscles   iss razor-sharp teeth   the growling
fucker made it over

big dog gives chase and little dog flies itself tight into the space
between the wall and the abandoned fridge that lay sideways
big dog tries to force his fat head into the space but can't fit   so
it juss barks and screams at little dog who burss into tears   this
lasts the whole afternoon   little dog cramped in there   and big
dog patrolling up and down the fridge trying to figure out a way
of getting to little dog   then big dog's owner come home and
calls big dog inside so it returns to iss garden and goes in   but
after the day of torment little dog is so shook that it don't come
out from behind the fridge   it juss stay there clutching iss little
chest with iss little paws till it hears iss owner's keys jingle to
open the garden door   then little dog darts indoors   skids
across the laminate   and throws isself behind the kitchen bin
where it has one feverish cry   then later on   iss so cross at

doglife being not fair   that it chews up iss owner's shoe
shaking it round in a mad rage till it get neck ache   come the
next day   little dog is too shook to go garden   so it stays
indoors   and ends up pissing and shitting round the house
owner comes home to pure rankness   and cos little dog is
misbehaving and unlearning basic rules that got laid down early
on the grid   owner decides that from time to time he'll kick
little dog in iss bellyside   make it stop the foolishness

so now little dog can't get peace outdoors or in   and I watch
little dog as it come to iss garden window   and iss looking out
into the garden like it does now for hours   iss whining some
sad song to isself   a song about the time when big dog from
the next garden came over and ate him and he died   cos little
dog is depressed   and when you're depressed you imagine iss
worse than it is

so now what little dog hates most of all is iss big tail   it used to
love catching it moving through the side of iss eye   but now
when little dog sees it iss juss scary   iss big tail ain't that
different to big dog from the next garden's tail   so little dog
will catch it move in iss peripheral and run away from iss own
tail   reach the dark hiding place behind the bin   be calm there
then see the tail will rise up in the side of iss eye again   and
little dog gets stress and runs away again   this goes on and on
and little dog is juss getting crazier and crazier

I look all the way down past the phone box   where the beauty
shop is   where mrs blackwood been working many years
doing hair and beauty for women who all day talk about their
problems   nuff heads think mrs blackwood don't join in on the
talks cos she got her life in order   and nuff heads say   *I want
no stress like smiling blackwood   all this life havoc is alien to
smiling blackwood*   but deep inside mrs blackwood knows that
she muss have a problem   she's been carrying round some
heavy weight in her chest for a while now but don't know why

mum told me a couple years back   mum's in the beauty shop
waiting to get treatment   everyone's juss talking like normal
mrs blackwood's giving someone a treatment   but her mind is
drifting   and she keep staring at some women in the shop   but

only at the ones who in church mr blackwood rush to shake
hands with   the ones who at weddings mr blackwood would
have a one-on-one talk with outside or in a side room where
only children are   then she look over at marsha sat there
marsha who still comes by daily   mum's watching mrs
blackwood watch these women back and forth   and iss like
mrs blackwood is seeing suttin   a pattern   and my mum sees
the pattern   she sees it   all the women mr blackwood perks up
for have the same two tings in common

mrs blackwood goes to get lunch and mum watches her through
the window   as mrs blackwood walks round seeing for the first
time that all the women modelling clothes in the pictures in the
shop windows and all the women holding the perfumes on the
side of passing buses   have these two tings   then mrs
blackwood approaches the beauty shop and when she reaches she
nearly drops her container of lunch when she sees what she sees
right here in this beauty shop window   where she work   the
pictures of the women here and on the walls inside   all these
women all have the two tings   two tings that mrs blackwood
herself   ain't got   mum watches mrs blackwood she can't eat
her lunch this day   she can't think   mrs blackwood juss sits
there in a daze as the shop carries on as usual

then mrs blackwood asks herself a question   she asks it in her
head   however she wants to know the answer so bad that the
question don't stay in her head   it comes out her mouth   *am
I ugly*   in this packed-out beauty shop everyone juss shuts up
and freezes   mrs blackwood goes on and they all lissen   not
even saying   *but*   or   *amen*   they know to let her finish cos
when a woman who been quiet in this shop for twelve years
opens up her mouth iss gotta be for good reason   but outta mrs
blackwood's good reason comes badness like never before hail
down on this beauty shop   a whole hell of arguments open up
people's opinions split down the middle bout women with them
two tings

by the end of it all   some lifelong customers   say they ain't
stepping foot in the beauty shop again ever   this one says she
won't let this one touch her hair again ever   this hairdresser

threatens to go work at a next beauty shop if she don't get to
switch chair so she don't have to dress hair near this beautician
who has a different view about women with the two tings

mum heard that when the shop closed for the night   the lady
who owns the shop   who known mrs blackwood since they
were juss girls clapping eenie meenie miney mo and miss mary
mack mack mack   asks mrs blackwood to stay behind   *what's
all this madness you bring into work today   there's hatred in
your heart*   mrs blackwood juss stay frozen quiet and smiling
that smile till she suddenly she juss burss out crying like a little
girl   the owner hugs her   and mrs blackwood cries even
bigger   not cos it feels good to cry in her old friend's arms
but cos not only does she have a problem with women who
have them two tings   what's worse is that the shop owner   her
tightest girlfriend from early on the grid   has them two tings

the beauty shop gets most of iss business from doing tricks that
make women who don't naturally have them two tings appear to
have them two tings   but after all these years   mrs blackwood
ain't sure she can keep doing them tricks any more   in fact
she wishes she could traips back and undo them all

I look to gandhi's corner shop

whenever I'm in that shop he's always cussing stray cat
telling it how useless it is and how much respect he lost for it
cos even though he lock it in the shop overnight it still ain't
killed one rat over the years   all stray cat does is sleep on the
bread high high up on the top shelf   far away from the rats
who love bread

gandhi's disappointed that he ain't ever opened up the shop to
a dead rat   he's told me how many times he's tried to block the
holes with brillo pad and tin foil   but the rats still reach
through   *they have many routes* gandhi says   worse thing bout
rats is that instead of sharing one pack of crisps among them
they'll open six packs and yam juss a bit of each   gandhi feeds
the remainder to stray cat   and stray cat moves sluggish cos of
that   sometimes it don't wanna move at all   like when
gandhi's walking round the shop   he cusses it for not moving

out the way when he's walking up and down   he tells it that
one day   if it don't come out the way   he'll blast it into the air

I was in the shop the day gandhi finally phoned the rat-killers
they gave gandhi a quote that made him slam his nokia on the
counter so hard that the plastic face and rubber buttons came off
and the battery fell out   gandhi's mad and goes to storm off but
the cat's there in his way on the floor   these times gandhi ain't in
no mood to change the direction he's storming off in juss to avoid
stray cat   so he winds up his leg to boot it like he promised   but
then   at the last second he changes his mind and he walks as
normal   to give stray cat a chance to come out his way   only
stray cat don't come out his way   and with only a bit of his
weight gandhi steps on stray cat's leg   there's a crunch sound
like when you step on snail   then there's one mad scream from
stray cat   and it juss flies out the shop with a quickness

stray cat is the longest friend gandhi's ever kept and now iss
gone   as gandhi locks up his shop for the night he looks around
the bins   but his friend ain't there   and he says to himself   *ah
well   lousy stray ting should've come out my way*

next morning gandhi opens up shop   and when stray cat ain't
there to jump down from the high high bread and bow to him
gandhi feels a hot flush behind his eyes that he wasn't expecting
and he nearly cries   he misses it   he feels a tightness in his
chest the whole day   he sits in a trance reminiscing all the
good times he and stray cat had together   gandhi misses stray
cat so bad that that evening   when the ting limps back into his
shop   gandhi hurdles over the till   and pops open a fresh pack
of plantain chips for stray cat   then he stacks boxes of drink
together in the shape of stairs so stray cat can still go up to sleep
on the high high bread

it drags itself up to the bread   licks iss leg for a while but the
leg won't get better   the what what girls come in the shop and
they don't teef no more   they buy tobacco and rizla now   and
they buss up at stray cat's leg bending the wrong way   gandhi
don't know how they can be so cruel   he's all stressing over it
but the what what girls been telling gandhi to his face   *what
you've earned the stress   you ain't no nice man   don't fink*

we've forgotten   you're a murderer a poor man died cos of you
you killed off old man boateng   letting youts buy drink for him
all dem years   helping the poor man stay as drunk as possible
fuck your cat

I watch them what what girls leave gandhi's shop and head over
to them smoking boys   they're always rolling with each other
now   some what what girls sitting on some smoking boys' laps
or sitting on a moped like a couple   always on the road
together   there's a connection they got and iss more than the
fact they're all sick of fighting their parents for the remote
something deeper connecting them   comes from a place of loss
and they fill up that hole for each other   so they're all at the
corner of trevor senior's house   nuff of them   some leaning
on his wall   like iss their wall

trevor senior and trevor junior out there practising   practising
likesay they don't know that it's too late to for trevor junior to
become a banging cricketer now   likesay people trevor junior's
age still get scouted   likesay by now it ain't juss a pipe dream
they practise hard and ignore the smoking and cussing

the ball rolls over to the smoking boys and trevor junior moves
to get it back   but the smoking boys pick it up and start playing
piggy in the middle   trevor junior running from side to side
the smoking boy with his hoodie on backwards is the main
joker who's mocking

trevor senior calmly walking over   *come on you lot   stop the*
foolishness   come on oi   but they carry on and trevor senior
can see his son is bout to cry   cheek twitching   lip wobbling
so trevor senior juss loses it and grabs the red cricket bat like
before   and he runs at the smoking boy with the hoodie on
backward like before   he swings the bat at him like before
but unlike before   the smoking boy don't run   and from here
I see the smoking boy juss fall forward   hit the ground   and
not move   it looked like the bat juss clipped him   a little clip
but the way them smoking boys and what what girls react
maybe it was more than juss a clip

they dash trevor senior gainst the wall   blast him   jump on
him   stamping on him like when you're trying to pop an empty

ribena carton   neighbours who try to stop it get slam to the
pavement and swung into each other   police and ambulance
come   the smoking boys run   trevor junior got his hands on
his head cos he can't believe it   snot run down his lips   tears
drop from his chin   ambulance taking trevor senior away cos
his eyes are swollen shut   but he's all trying to break away
from the ambulance men   blood coming out his mouth as he's
trying to explain to the police that the smoking boys started it
you're five years late   he's telling them   *five years too late*

the ambulance take trevor senior away   and the smoking boy
with the hoodie on backward ain't moved this whole time   he
gets wheeled off too   police put tape round the corner of the
road   but I still see blood on the floor that had poured from the
boy's head   and white popcorns on the floor that came out of
trevor senior's mouth

behind me mum opens the balcony door and says I gotta go
shop for her   she looks nuff old man   started sending me
gandhi's every day

I'm in the shop   mrs blackwood come in the shop and say to
me   *ain't seen your mum in a while   she ain't been salon or
been church or been the same since the miscarriage   I know
it's been years but we don't forget   please tell her come talk to
me we'll pray together*   nobody's seen how bad she's gotten
except jamilla

I get home and jamilla's at my door   police still on the corner
we go inside   mum's completely stopped cooking now juss sits
round drinking   so iss all me now   jamilla helps sometimes
with the bigger events when I can't do it alone   she's not my
girl   she don't even really speak to me when she's here helping
sometimes she'll go   *how much of this do I use*   but thass it

we're cooking now and the kitchen's nuff small   whenever we
get close to each other   she turns her body away so we don't
touch   sometimes we smoke on the balcony after cooking and if
she feels lucky enough she lets me put my arm around her   but
thass rare   I'm staring at her   her eczema's all gone now   she
don't smell of b o no more   even though the what what girls still

cuss her for it when they see her   she's pretty   she ain't skinny
like before   her legs are long and whenever she wears this skirt
I wanna do things that I know she won't lemme

we finish cooking and I walk jamilla to the train station
always do   iss my rule   we could walk it but she likes taking
the overground   iss only one stop   but she's into trains   she
loves trains man

I cut through the market on my way back and iss juss shutting
but I buy meat in time   I stop outside sam's bike shop I don't
know if I should go in or not cos sam's been moving booky
every time I go in there he's screwing up his face at me   like
last week I tried to step into his shop and sam came running to
the front and pushed the door shut

then locked it and flipped the *we're closed* sign   don't know
why sam did that   cos I never steal anything   maybe he was
closing early that day

anyway I'm outside his shop now   and I go to step inside
when the same thing happens again juss like last week   sam
comes running to close the door on me   I hold it open this time
we're both wrestling with the door   him wanting to close it and
me wanting to come in   iss a gridlock cos we're the same
strength   we're both growling and I ask sam   whass your
problem with me sam   sam says   *you can't be in my shop no*
more son   why's dat   *you making my customers upset*   I don't
even chat to your customers   *one of them complained*   I ain't
never done nothing in your shop but look at the bikes and
squeeze a break lever or a padded seat from time to time sam so
I don't know what a customer even got to complain bout   *the*
smell   come again sam   *it bothers them and it bothers me and*
I can smell it right now   what you on bout   *the raw meat and*
stinky fish you always bring in here   *stinks out my shop long*
after you're gone

my arm buckles   sam strong-arms the door and I stumble back
he locks it   flips the *closed* sign   then goes to the back and
carries on fixing a bike there   I stand feeling like some
dickhead looking through the glass   what juss happened dint

need to happen   if sam juss told me before I'd have stopped
bringing my meat in his shop   instead it comes to this and man
push me out his shop   and expects me to hold the hit   but
I know better than to carry this feeling around with me

I notice the rusty the bike   this one that sam keeps on display
out here leaning on the glass   well sam pushed me   so I push
the rusty bike   away   I wheel rusty down the street with me
the back wheel squeaks when it rotates   tyres are flat too

I'm wheeling it home   when I notice a brudda on the other side
of the road   wheeling a rusty bike too   he raises his chin to
me   and when we pass each other   I remember that it was
right here   exactly here   where I passed that duppy a few
years back   who was juss like me   that was him   that was the
duppy   I turn around to look at it   but iss riding off on iss
rusty bike   and I fully would've gone after it   if I knew how
to ride mine

six

so I'm riding down my road and iss not what it used to be   iss
quieter   the smoking boys and what what girls ain't come back
to the corner for some time after the incident   the boy with the
hoodie on backward dint die though   but parently when trevor
senior went court for what he done   the boy with the hoodie on
backwards' family wheel him in to the courtroom   the boy
don't speak properly any more   parently the boy dribbles like
a baby   parently when trevor senior takes the stand to explain
what a god-fearing man he is and how he's juss trying to do
good for trevor junior parently every now and then smoking
boy in his wheelchair giggles and claps like a baby   parently it
makes trevor senior buss into tears   not able to finish what he's
saying   parently security have to remove trevor senior from the
courtroom cos you're not allowed to speak all the time in courts
and trevor senior couldn't stop crying and saying   *I'm sorry*
I'm sorry I'm sorry

I ride pass trevor junior he juss sits there on the corner alone
no bat no ball   cos the dream went away when his dad did   he
got reality now   he juss sits there staring into space *slow down*
jamilla says   she's behind me   she taught me how to ride a
few months back   so now after we cook   instead of taking her
straight to the train station we ride about a bit first   rusty's old
so squeaks a lot and her tyres need pumping all the time but iss
still worth it cos   all the turning corners and going over bumps
means jamilla has to hold and grab me a lot   I mount the curb
at full speed and gandhi's limping stray cat is in front of us   iss
doing it again   it ain't gonna get out our way   I make a hard
swerve so I don't run into it   but rusty skids and jamilla and
I fall and slide across the pavement sideways

my jeans are torn but I'm fine   jamilla though she's wearing
a skirt   so her knee took a nasty scrape on the gravel   I ride
us back to mine   rusty's back wheel squeaks sadly   in my room

I put jamilla's knee on my leg   I wipe her cut with a stingy wipe
thingy   I'm putting the plaster on her knee   and I can feel it I
know jamilla can feel it too   on the back of her knee   through
my jeans juss rising up   I look at the skin on her thighs   I take
my mind to the middle of these thighs and imagine what iss like
there   my hand got a mind of iss own and juss goes to her thigh
I don't even know when I put it up her skirt but this is what we're
dealing with now   we've never even kissed   and I got my hand
here   jamilla's making a breathing sound   she's not saying
anything but she ain't moving away from me   now I know what
to do from here cos I've seen it on tv   I pull her knickers off I get
on top of her   I slide myself inside her   but what happens now
I dint see on tv   jamilla goes crazy   pushes me off of her   goes
mental   clothes back on   runs out my room   runs out my yard

I follow her train station   she walks and I ride behind cos I feel
bad   her train comes and she goes   but the way she kicked me
off of her   I don't know when next I'll see her   I go home
after bout an hour the bell rings   I'm shook as I go to open the
door cos I juss know iss jamilla's dad come to have a go at me
I open up and iss jamilla by herself   she goes straight to my
room   wraps her legs around my back   and we do it   then we
do it again couple hours later   and she stays over   she's asleep
beside me   and I smile   cos I'm slyly glad the stray cat's
broke leg made us fall

come morning we're still in bed when jamilla starts properly
speaking to me   telling me bout trains   that she has a train set
at home that she's played with since early on the grid   that
some afternoons she rides the silverlink all the way to barking
then catches it back the other way   she's talking so much about
trains that I fall back asleep   I wake up and she's still going on
about trains

we get up and we cook and iss fun now cos she lets me touch
her   I put music on and we dance like fools and copy each
other   but she drops an egg on the floor   so I flick some batter
on her   she dashes a seasoned chicken drumstick at me   but
I duck it and then dunk the bowl we marinated the fish in on her
head   *not taking it off your head less you kiss me*   she kisses
me hard on the lips cos she kisses nuff hard   I shampoo the fish

smell out of her hair   I ride her station   she steps forward
when the trains coming cos she likes to feel it blow past her
likes to watch the mice scatter when the tracks rumble

come the next day we do the same again   and the same after
that   some months go by and we're cooking most days these
times   cos the food we make is good   and cos people marry
and people die   we do wake keepings engagement parties
birthdays baby showers   thass decent money   and since mum
don't help with anything   I juss give her a third of what we
make   the rest I split with jamilla

we've got so good at cooking together now that jamilla don't
need to ask how much of this or that to use   we juss cook and
dance to the music   then go smoke on the balcony   then do
the ting in my room   then ride rusty around

we're in my room and jamilla hands me her share of the money
she's made me hold it for her from the beginning   she don't say
iss cos her dad might get to it but she don't have to   I save all of
mine too   we keep it together in a pillowcase that I hide behind
my chest of drawers   but we pour it all out today though   cos
we wanna throw it around the room like we're rich and lie in it
like they do on tv   we're lying there now   money under us and
all around us   *what we gonna do with it   I mean   I like our life
I don't wanna change it up I wanna cook with you forever   look
at this   when we put these notes back in the pillowcase it
reaches the middle of the case   what if when the notes reach the
top of the pillowcase   and there's enough in there to rest your
head on it and use it like a pillow   without saying bye or see ya
later to anyone   what if we juss jump on one of them big trains
that neither of us have been on yet   take it to the last stop   and
where ever that is   we open up the pillowcase and open up a
shop there   people from that area will walk past our shop   and
smell the curry goat and jollof rice   and stew chicken and egusi
soup   and they'll come in   look up at the menu   ask what a
buss-up shot is   we'll give them likkle sample   taste a likkle
sample   they'll lick their lips   and beg us to fill up one two
container for them to take home to family*

thass the plan   thass the plan

everything jamilla and I do from here on is going to the shop

iss afternoon   I leave jamilla there cooking so I can go buy some ingredients we're running low on   I wheel rusty out on to the road and I see trevor junior   I see him sat on the corner smoking   doing the thing his dad hated the smoking boys for doing   I wonder how trevor senior would feel   knowing he's gone prison juss so his son can put down the cricket and replace the smoking boys

couple neighbours often go to see trevor junior there on that corner   and me   I ride over to him   cos trevor junior got that ting to top up the lucky feeling   and he's always there to sort you out

I ride past mrs blackwood who's taking out her rubbish   she don't look the same   parently a few weeks back some products start going missing from the beauty shop   it happens to be the same products mrs blackwood refuses to use on people any more because of the two tings   there's no evidence but they all reckon mrs blackwood is pouring it down the drain   most people in the beauty shop have made peace and don't care bout the two tings any more   or as mrs blackwood tells them   *iss not that you don't care iss that you're in denial hunny*   then she goes in the back and more products go missing   I cycle pass her and she looks kinda crazy now   her smile is mad wide with her eyes nuff open as she waves to me   parently no customers wanted to go to mrs blackwood's chair for treatments any more cos they say the talk that blackwood talk is too stressful   so mrs blackwood is asked to give up her chair for someone who can draw customers

so with mrs blackwood home all hours marsha don't come over with her washing like before   but people say her and mr blackwood still linking up   cos mr blackwood leaves for his night shift earlier every evening now   and gets back in the afternoon instead of morning now

as I ride past mrs blackwood I notice something   she's still smiling but she looks nuff different   it seems that mrs blackwood has started to have those two tings   and the thought

in my head is that maybe   maybe those products that went
missing from the beauty shop dint go down the drain   maybe
mrs blackwood was taking them home   maybe she gave in
and started using them on herself   thinking that having them
two tings might get her mr blackwood back

on the ride back from market I'm nuff dreamy in my own world
cos   I got everything I want   I got rusty   I got jamilla   and
now I got our restaurant to look forward to   I'm juss cruising
down the road past a group of them smoking boys and what
what girls when I hear one of them call me out of my name
it ain't the normal chicken-boy thing they cuss me about for
having bags of meat balancing on both handle bars   iss a proper
call-out   and I know iss at me cos nobody else is passing I stop
and look round to see who it is calling me a teef   the brudda
steps forward   calls me a teef again   of all the smoking boys
I've seen I don't recognise this one   till he says   *I heard you
took my trainers off me   come and take them again if you're
bad*   desmon   one next

brudda comes to desmon's side now   massive martin   he's
even bigger   it ain't fat no more though pure muscle   desmon
takes his trainers off and puts them on the floor   *come take
them innit*   the smoking boys snicker and dare me to take them
I juss put my middle finger up and I ride off

I duck into gandhi's to get seasoning   gandhi got a no-bike
policy so I lean rusty against the window with the meat on the
handle bars and gandhi keeps an eye on it like normal   I'm
getting the seasoning when gandhi starts yelling and hitting the
glass   I run outside   my meat   is poured out onto the
pavement and rusty is being rode away   not even fast
desmon's juss riding it away slow   he don't even throw a look
over his shoulder to check if I'm coming after him   iss like he
knows I ain't gonna do nuffin   iss like we're at school again
come like I'm getting tie-walked

I get indoors   jamilla and I keeping cooking   there's no dance
and joke cos I ain't in the mood   jamilla takes two hundred out
the pillow   *go buy a new one*   I put the money back cos   *this
is for our shop I don't wanna buy a new one thass not the point*

the point is he's doing it again   but it ain't the same like how it
was before

I take jamilla station   she gets on the train   the doors are
closing and I can see someone running down the stairs to catch
it   if I put out my hand the doors'll stop closing   I can hold it
open for this person running   there's enough time   but rusty
got took today   I ain't in the mood to be kind to strangers   the
doors close and the train pulls away   and I walk past the guy
who tried to catch it   shit   iss the duppy   deep down I know
I should've held the door   but my mood is too rotten to care

coming out the station I hear rusty's back wheel squeaking
desmon rides straight past me   *oi*   he stops   I go to him   my
throat feels shaky so I know not to say anything   I juss put my
shaky hand on rusty's handle bar   desmon shouts in my face
pushes me to the floor   then he does it again riding away slow
without even a look back like he knows I won't do nothing   so
I get up I run at him   I juss mow him down with everything in
me   he smacks the floor   I drag up my bike   I ride away   the
tyres are flat   iss moving slow   desmon's getting up and
shouting at me   he's coming   running   running faster than
rusty's riding   so I buss a left back into the train station   rusty
gets caught when I try pull her over the barrier with me   I don't
wanna leave her   but desmon's in the station now   I hear a train
on the platform   I hear the beeping of the doors closing   I leave
rusty and run for it   behind me   desmon jumps the barrier and
shouts what he's gonna do to me when he catches me   I see the
train doors closing   I jump down the last few steps and run   but
the doors all close at the same time   desmon's coming down the
last few stairs when I see it   a few carriages down there's a light
from a carriage door thass still open   I dash to it   I see a hand
holding it open as I throw myself on   the doors close juss as
desmon gets to it   he looks at me through the glass   I look at
him   he punches the glass as the train pulls away

the duppy   he held the door open for me   what I dint do for
him   the duppy goes and sits down   I nod to him   he raises
his chin at me

come morning I go to buy my ting off trevor junior as I'm
walking away he tells me   *desmon and them smoking boys
looking for you   stay home let it cool over*   I hit the balcony
smoke too much trying not to think about it   all them feelings
coming back   *from time you ain't nevah headlock no one you
get tret this way*

jamilla comes and I don't speak less she ask me something
she keeps asking me the same thing   I keep telling her iss
nothing   she slides her fingers in mine   I don't grip it   she
asks if I'm awake   I don't open my eyes   don't answer   so
she goes home   but I can't sleep   all I can do is think I ain't
letting him win over me again

iss early morning and I go over to trevor junior on the corner
juss to tell him   oi tell desmon I wanna fight him one on one
juss normal me and him   I go back home and I wait   I box in
the living room   this is the only way   to make him know what
a headlock feels like from the inside   few hours go by I look
over the balcony and no smoking boys are there   gotta start
cooking and jamilla ain't reach yet   I message her   *where are
you*   no reply   I cook alone   I check my phone   no replies
when I walk to the station I clock some smoking boys across
the road   they all stop talking as they watch me go by
desmon ain't with them   I watch the rats scatter when the
tracks rumble   I ring jamilla's doorbell   I sit on her bedside
I ask why she's crying   she shows me

I ask who done it

I ask if it was only them

I go home and smoking boys are on the corner of trevor's house
bout twenty of them stood   trevor junior with them   he wags
his head to me telling me not to come over   I'm juss stood here
looking   desmon's sat on the wall looking straight back at me
he smiles then says   *how's b o girl*   the smoking boys don't let
me get near when I go for him   they push me back   then hit me
till I fall   blast me when I'm down there   my head's on the
concrete while I'm taking these licks   I close my eyes   trying to

make sense of it   being good dint make mrs blackwood or old
man boateng feel good   and look where passing on the hit got
trevor senior   neither of them work   I lissen for my dad's voice
but he got nuttin to say   nuttin works

seven

people are still getting married and having babies and dying   the
world don't stop cos of us   I go meet jamilla at the station   iss
the first time we're gonna cook since it happened   and I decide
to walk her from station to mine   I don't want her walking
through the area alone no more   we hear a car beep   fiat punto
across the road   parked up   smoking boys and what what girls
stood round it   desmon's elbow out the window   he's smiling
desmon turns to the what what girls   laughs something to them
bout jamilla   the girls ain't laughing with him   they're juss
staring at jamilla   guilt   shame   in their eyes   jamilla can't
look at them   she cries as we walk   I try hold her hand but she
don't want that

we cook   she won't let me touch her   iss like how it was
before   she don't speak to me no more   no music   we go to
my room   holding her   it ain't easy   she's   she's stopped
eating   iss like holding someone else   what happened to her
she's broken

the pillowcase   it ain't full but we're three quarters there
I think we should go tomorrow   jump on a train like we said
without telling anyone juss go   there's probably enough to get
a small shop   we'll start off small   jamilla smiles   first smile
I see from her since   she nods   she kisses me soft   she offers
herself to me for the first time in a while   and iss not that
I don't want to   I been wanting to be this close to her again but
I can't stop myself from thinking bout what happened   when
she went station that night   alone   cos I dint walk her   cos
I dint wanna run into desmon   cos I was shook   how the what
what girls grabbed her   how them girls did what desmon
ordered them to   pinned my jamilla down   tore her shirt open
sprayed her up   sprayed up her body   till the cans were done
and juss spraying out air   till her skin was burnt and frosted
and disfigured   I'm on top of jamilla and   I'm looking at her
body   I don't know if it'll ever heal up properly

I lie beside her   cos I can't do it   she rubs my neck   tells me
iss ok   hugs me   I keep my head in her chest so she don't see
me crying   this had nuttin to do with her   iss meant to be
between me and desmon   iss my fault this happened to her
I say to her   *let's go tonight   I don't see why we should wait
let's go now*

I pack the pillowcase and a bag   mum's asleep on the sofa
I go to her   kiss her gently

we're walking station to go jamilla's for her stuff   she needs to
eat she's walking nuff slow   we pass the betting shop
jamilla's dad in there on his knees forehead to the floor   can't
tell if he's weeping or kissing the ground   jamilla blows him
a kiss even though he don't see us

the mice run away when the tracks rumble   we're finally
getting out of here   she comes forward to feel the breeze of the
train passing like she always does   but she's weak   and she
juss goes slowly   forward   in the side of my eye   I see her
fall forward   slowly   the train comes

eight

I'm on the balcony   smoking   ash blows on to dad's black suit
I'm wearing   the funeral will have started by now   I don't get
the whole coffin thing   who's it fooling   iss for when
someone's stayed a certain shape   if anything juss don't have
a coffin   don't have one   cos having one there   juss reminds
me of what I know is actually in there

at the cemetery   I'm stood near the gate where I can smoke
this without no one chatting to me   see a few people from
school there   her dad says a prayer   mum's juss there   I keep
this distance cos I don't wanna see no one   I don't want the
side of my arm rubbed by short elderly women calling me son
I juss watch from here till everyone's gone   then I go to her

you was juss here jamilla   we dint even finish our last convo
we had plans girl   we were meant to do the shop together

in the distance I see that same duppy brudda   he's at a grave
paying respects to someone he knew   he comes over   we juss
stand looking at jamilla's grave for a while   I got a little toy
train in my hand   but I can't put it down

I go home and back on the balcony with a smoke and I still got
this train in my hand   I look down and watch it all happening
nuff smoking boys and what what girls crowd at the corner   iss
their corner now   a few of them wearing their hoodie on
backward with the hood on the chest like that boy used to do
one of dem got the big dog from that garden on a leash   letting
it terrorise people passing

desmon comes and they all quieten down   not out of respect
but out of fear   trevor junior and I still talk   he told me that
what happened to jamilla none of them agreed with it   the girls
dint even wanna do it but desmon force them   he told me how
iss pure wickedness what desmon does   punched up one

smoking boy for having ideas different to him   teefed a next
one's what what girl and told him to relax that he'll give her
back when finish   starting trouble with other areas for no
reason   parently nuff of them lot don't support it   nuff of
them talk behind his back now   thass what trevor junior says
but I watch from here and they smiling to his face

I see mum down there still wearing the black dress   since
I stop going gandhi's for her she has to go buy the ting herself
now iss all out in the open and everyone knows what she is
she's out there on the bench daily with some others   drinking
and mumbling

I see mrs blackwood   that woman ain't smiling no more   she
look rough   her hair looking wild   she looks half-and-half like
she kinda had those two tings but ain't topped up on them in a
while   maybe them products run out   or maybe she's given up
on it cos she remembered iss juss a trick

mrs blackwood puts bins out   she's wearing one nightgown
that show so much arm that it show a portion of sidebreast too
she see marsha across the road sitting in her doorway catching
some sun while being on the phone   mrs blackwood shouts
something to her about women who don't cross their legs when
they're sitting   marsha comes off the phone telling mrs
blackwood   *repeat what you say if you bad*   and mrs
blackwood tells marsha how she can see marsha's wide bucket
all the way from where she standing   they both run at each
other meeting in the middle of the road to commence pulling
each other's hair   smoking boys what what girls and all the
neighbours watching   mrs blackwood and marsha bouncing off
a car setting off the alarm   banging their fist on each other's
head like they're shaking maracas   till some smoking boys
come and tear them apart   marsha's face got red lines across it
and mrs blackwood's half-and-half hair is blowing in the wind
the nightgown she got on got tug so baggy   that what iss
letting be shown juss ain't right

mrs blackwood goes in her yard   starts dashing mr
blackwood's clothes out from the top window   oh now mr
blackwood comes home   but she's locked the door from the

inside   she shouts down at him   expects him to beg or
something   but he's calm juss picking up his clothes patting
out the dust and folding it   it makes her madder and she tries to
spit on him   she tells people passing that the man is worthless
he's a pathetic individual   tells mr blackwood to go live with
that ting across the road   so marsha opens her door   mr
blackwood goes to marsha

now mrs blackwood has changed clothes   she walks across to
marsha's door   asks marsha calmly   *what did I ever do to you
marsha why did you take my man*   marsha's saying nuff calmly
back   *you kicked him out mrs blackwood you don't want him*
mrs blackwood come with   *yeah but swear down you took him
long before that though marsha you open up your leg for him
when you know he's marry and love up his wife*   this makes
marsha laugh   *a joke this muss be cos when's the larss time he
say he love you*   mrs blackwood don't have a good backchat
for that so she starts another boxing match   round two   the
smoking boys don't stop it this time cos they got bets riding on
it   mrs blackwood and marsha do battle till both of them are
too tired to carry on   mrs blackwood with her patchy head
marsha with her scratched-up neck   both of them on the floor
crying   blaming each other for the way things are

I look to gandhi's shop   gandhi's dad is outside the shop about
to jump into a cab   his dad finally came to visit gandhi but he's
leaving now   I don't reckon gandhi's sad to see the old man go
it wasn't the type of visit gandhi had in mind   every time I was
in the shop all gandhi's dad did was juss was follow gandhi round
cussing him   telling him he don't do nuttin properly   and
cussing him bout the stray cat saying   *you've never had brains
pritish*   thass his name   *pritish you should be like your younger
brothers they use their head   look at these picture   of their
beautiful wives   standing around in some of their apartments
why dint you lissen when I was raising you   the offer from your
brothers is still open   they still want you to join the company
start from the bottom like they did*   the visit from his dad made
gandhi so stressed that man had a stroke   I watch him with the
walking stick help his dad with his luggage   and all now as his
dad's getting in the cab still saying   *you brought this on yourself*

*I've never had a stroke and I'm eighty   why are you having a
stoke   iss cos you don't lissen   even your body is telling you
that you are wrong*

gandhi shuts the cab door and is glad to see the cab pull away
and behind him there's the *jingle jingle* sound   some new
young nah nah girls teefing up his shop   gandhi don't rush
back to the shop though   he juss stroll back   cos whass the
point   he's worked nuff hard on the corner shop all this time
and whass he got to show   his big idea to make his dad proud
ain't work   and he himself don't know what he's gained from
life   he's juss confused   so he lets them steal   he pretends to
be mad at them when he catches them do it   but deep down
he ain't mad   he's juss sad

I see down at the corner   my mum's stumbling around   she
falls over   desmon and them lot laugh at her   she pulls herself
on to the bench and cusses desmon out   now desmon sends
one of the younger smoking boys to buy a couple beers for her
he gives it to her   and now mum and him are friends
laughing with each other   like he ain't the reason she's in a
black dress right now

they're all looking up now   looking right at me   my mum's
juss stood there with her hand over her mouth   mrs blackwood
and marsha and mr blackwood and trevor junior clocking me
big dog barking up at me   desmon staring at me   smoking his
ting and staring at me   I know what he's saying I can see it in
his eyes   and thass why I do what I do   I climb back down off
the balcony wall   go to my room   mum comes in to cuss me
out   I cry till I'm asleep

I wake up   I hear sirens   and nuff people shouting   from the
balcony I see that everyone's down the road   crowded by the
main road   near gandhi's   and near the beauty shop   mum
left the tv on   news says a brudda was kilt by police   kilt by
police yesterday   and now the community ain't having it any
more   they ain't taking it   cos this brudda is far from the first
cos this brudda is yet another   an the police story keep
changing   they said he shot a gun   that it was a shoot-out
now they say it wasn't   but that he had a gun   and iss like it

always is   not making enough sense   cos they covering suttin
up   they show the young brudda's face

somehow I juss knew

iss him   the duppy   who held the door open for me   I saw
him this morning at the cemetery   been dead since yesterday

I hit the road and iss pure madness   pure anger in every eye
police dogs barking at us   nuff heads shouting   mr blackwood
is shouting   *they've done it again   they keep killing us and*
getting away with it   police meant to be protecting us   but
who protects us from you   who will protect us from you   I
ain't saying the brudda was a saint   I dint know him   but I'm
saying you don't kill your own people the way you kill us   and
when all's said and done   you walk away with it   no police
officer has ever been done for killing in this country   how's
that   not one   not one charge has stuck   you lot are killing
for free man   you lot got licence to kill   tell me how dass fair
how lot been getting away with murder   it ain't new   this ain't
news   fuck all of you lot   fuck the police   fuck the police
fuck the police   fuck the police   fuck the police

people phlegming them   lobbing things at them   things are
flying over my head   but it feels safe on this side

nuff smoking boys and what what girls buzzin   they got
hoodies on backward   they've pulled the hood up now   over
their face   got the eyes cut out   they were ready iss like they
knew this day was coming   then I spot him   juss there   and
suddenly I can't seem to hear the crowd any more   all I see is
the back of his head   massive martin and a couple smoking
boys stood near him   hoodies on backward but I know them
well   I see their eyes   they see me coming for him   they know
whass in my mind   cos they see the brick in my hand   but they
don't make a move to me   and they don't tell desmon   they
ain't gonna stop me today   they turn away   massive martin
turns his back   I'm right behind desmon now   I raise the brick
up   so I can end it all   you can flick my ear and kick my chair
but I'm caving your head in now

something's caught my eye   something ahead of us

we're facing the riot   iss all silently happening right in front of
us   red cricket bat that I ain't seen in a while   swinging
trevor junior out there   a scarf masking his face   he swings
the bat into a police car   blowing out the windows   whass got
me watching him hard though is his face   he's loving it   he's
in a trance   ain't see him this happy since them first days I see
him and trevor senior practising   look at him   hitting back
I get what he's doing   he dents the roof in   pulls the door back
till it snaps and scrapes the floor

and further down on the other side of the street   I see this bald-
headed man   who's going mental   I keep looking   and I see
that nah it ain't a man   iss a bald-head woman   a woman
I recognise   she dashes a brick through the beauty shop
window   mrs blackwood   iss her   she juss dashes one fire
bottle into the beauty shop   she's cheering the blaze   cheering
the fire spreading in there   the owner of the shop   mrs
blackwood's good friend from day   is over by the side there
a small group of women with rollers still in their hair hold the
owner back and tell her   *iss not worth it owner   look at her
head she gone crazy man   what you gonna gain from mashing
up a mad person*   and mrs blackwood juss keep enjoying and
cheering   smiling that smile   she dashes a next fire bottle
but this time on to the display on the bus   of a half-naked
woman who got them two tings   holding up one perfume   of
which the perfume bottle is in the shape of how an attractive
woman's body apparently should be   she dashes the fire bottle
for all the flat-chested women   and for the ones who have too
much chest   mrs blackwood's bald head sweating   from all
the dancing and celebrating she's doing   as she watches the
image on the bus with flames curling up it

and juss past her is jamilla's dad   he dashes and redashes one
metal pole   into the william hill window   shattering it   he
sticks the pole in the shattered window and bends it around
till police take him down and draipss him away

I see mum   my mum there   stood still   a fire bottle in her
hand   stood there   looking at it   gandhi's corner shop
gandhi on his walking stick is trying to quickly close his shop

he got an eye on my mum   telling her not to do what she's
thinking about doing   reminding her how good he's been to her
nuff desperation in his eyes   he tries to pull his shutters down
but today's the day he's finally shrunk too short to reach   he
runs and gets a stool   wagging his finger at mum   he clambers
on to the stool and pulls down one shutter   talking over his
shoulder to my mum   she's juss stood there   gandhi takes his
stool to the second shutter now to pull it down   some
policemen there at the side now   not wanting to get too close
to mum   telling her to put it down   but they got their sticks in
their hand   the look on their faces as inch closer to her   if she
dashes it she's catching licks and she's getting nicked   I don't
even clock when I'm at mum's side now   I'm there cos I know
why she's gotta do it   but for some reason she's not doing it
she's letting the chance go   gandhi pulls the second shutter
down   I take the bottle from mum   them policemen shouting
something   gandhi runs inside   I take the lighter off mum
and gandhi's pulling hard   pulling on that stubborn slow door
I light the ting and I dash the ting   the fire bottle flies over
gandhi's head   goes in his shop   smashes   and the whole
place lights up behind him   he runs out the shop   puts his
hand on his head and his walking stick drops   he starts pulling
out his beard watching everything in his shop go orange and
black   them policemen pile on me   lock my arms behind my
back   but I can't feel the pain over all this good feeling
they're dragging me away   gandhi's run back into his burning
shop   man's gonna die in that shop of his   police don't go
after him thass not their job   the flames just get bigger and
blacker   then gandhi comes stumbling out with stray cat in his
arms   and where a minute ago he nearly had another stroke
watching his shop burn down   now gandhi's smiling   stroking
stray cat   kissing iss head   happy his friend is alive

nine

eighteen months wasn't bad

trevor junior came to visit me   told me I had desmon where nuff
people wanted him and could've done whatever I wanted to him
parently nuff people were mad at me for walking away   I dint
know this at the time but when I walked away I dropped the brick
and desmon clocked what I was gonna do to him   and as I was
walking   he picked up the brick   and was coming up behind me
to do me something   but they got in his way   the what what
girls   and when he pushed them out the way mr blackwood
stepped up to him   and when he dashed mr blackwood aside
the smoking boys grabbed desmon   dragged him off somewhere
dealt with him   and we ain't gonna see desmon again

I'm back home and I'm looking off the balcony   this the area
I'm from   we ain't perfect but we make sense to each other
I look down and see it all happening   things don't look too
different but it feels different   problems are still here cos
trouble is never done   but problems think twice before they
step to us now   cos we're harder now   tougher than we was
we hit back

mrs blackwood   she's been busy   cos some nineteen-year-old
dropped one baby to her door   saying iss mr blackwood who's
the father   and she ain't caring for it cos she got into uni   so
marsha who thought she was the only other woman blackwood
had eyes for kicks him out   mrs blackwood takes him back in
and now they're like   a family   baby and all   I know iss mad
but   I watch the three of them there in their doorway and I get
it   who are we to say whass right when we got nuff problem of
our own

the sound of cricket is back too cos trevor senior's back   out
there playing with trevor junior   they ain't playing for keeps
this time though   juss the joy of it   some of the smoking boys

join in with the cricket   and they still argue sometimes   so it
ain't all good   but it ain't all bad either

mum ain't drank this whole time   all the cooking has kept her
away from it   she's cooking again   she was always much
better at it than me   she feels good now   she got real
happiness inside her   the one where you're happy with what
you got   she got herself   I'm juss a bonus she says   and I
agree thass how it should be with me and her   some people
gotta love themself first   and thass ok

the pillow has been hidden behind my drawers this whole time
I go to the kitchen where mum's cooking   I pour all the money
out on the floor   mum thinks I've robbed a bank   *nah mum
we saved it me and jamilla   I got an the idea   let's we buy
gandhi's old corner shop   I know we the ones who bunn it
down   but dont you think iss perfect   for a takeout   we'll do
it up   we'll call it   jamilla's   think bout it   smoking boys
and what what girls coming to order and to complain bout us
taking too long to make it and marsha orders then complains
bout the portion size   what do you think*

oh and little dog with the big tail   that dog   that was not a
little dog it just had growing to do the ting grew into iss big tail
and came to be quite a big massive bitch full grown   so she
gives birth to a litter   and as if she planned it   as she was nuff
big now after she gave birth   and as she was nuff strong now
from all the kickings she'd taken over the years from her owner
she jumps over into big dog's garden   attacks big dog
something savage   mauls it something vicious   way past
revenge   and both owners agree that that dog which once was
little   gotta get put down   but hear this   word around the vet
is she went to the vet's smiling on that fateful morning   she
knew she was there to get the gas   but was still smiling   with
her massive tongue hanging out   and wagging her tail   while
walking down the hall to get kilt   the dogs in the surrounding
cages were barking saying   *dead dog walking   thass a dead
dog right there*   and when one shaggy dog in a cage asks our
little dog   *oi why'd you do it*   our little dog juss nicely barks
to him   *I know what I did seems wrong to some of you dogs*

and I know nuff dogs'll judge me   but what I did   was right
to me   it was right to me y'understand   anyone can be a good
dog   juss follow the rules and the guidelines and you'll be
a good dog   but being good and feeling good ain't the same
thing   you can be nuff good and feel not good   and thass what
was happening to me   I did what I done to feel ok about myself
again   cos feeling helpless is one of the worst ways a dog can
feel bout herself   I did it cos I dint wanna feel that way no
more   did it so my pups   their pups and pupses' pups after
can run free   chase tail in the garden   and take long
streaming   pisses   without some big dog ruining it

A Nick Hern Book

good dog first published in Great Britain in 2017 as a paperback original by Nick Hern Books Limited, The Glasshouse, 49a Goldhawk Road, London W12 8QP, in association with tiata fahodzi

Cover image: TEAfilms

Designed and typeset by Nick Hern Books, London
Printed and bound in Great Britain by Mimeo Ltd, Huntingdon, Cambridgeshire PE29 6XX

A CIP catalogue record for this book is available from the British Library

ISBN 978 1 84842 625 2